A Study Guide on

HOW TO WALK IN THE SPIRIT

By John Casteel, D. D.

2 4 6 8 10 9 7 5 3 1

ISBN 0-9748059-7-1

Book design and production: U. S. Press & Graphics, the Uncommon Printer

Cover design by U.S. Press & Graphics, the Uncommon Printer

Printed in the U.S.A., by U.S. Press & Graphics, the Uncommon Printer * Tucson, Arizona, www.uspress1.com

Contents

Introduction

These studies are designed to give the reader a glimpse of what is available to them in their relationship with the Holy Spirit, and to enable each person who reads them to experience the practical outworking of the Spirit in their own personal life.

The Holy Spirit's power is the only provision God has given us for daily and long term victory over sinful flesh. This was so in the days of the early Church and it is just as true today.

In fact the only answer for the believer's continual battle against the world, the flesh, and the devil, is to live and walk in the power of the Spirit, not just occasionally but in a daily experience. We must allow the Spirit of God to indwell us, empower us, and then lead us every day and in everything we do.

Obviously there is much more about this subject that I have yet to learn. Life in God is an ongoing process that will only be completed when we meet Him face to face. However, the principles that I share are proven by the Word of God, and in daily practice. They are not new ideas. They are the clear and powerful principles that have been given to us through the writings of the Apostles of the early Church. They are still powerful to guide those who trust God enough to surrender fully to Him, and let His Spirit continually reign in their human body, soul, and spirit.

We live in the last days. It is time for God's people to enter into their true destiny as overcomers. It is time for God's Church to become victorious over self and selfishness. Yet this can only take place one believer at a time as each one recognizes the folly of living according to the flesh and believes the promise of hope in the Holy Spirit.

All Scripture portions are taken from the New King James Version of the Holy Bible unless otherwise noted.

Chapter 1
Our Most Formidable Enemy

The Devil is not our most powerful adversary.

The most powerful enemy the believer faces is not the Devil or his demons. It is his or her sinful flesh that causes most of the problems.

The "flesh" is that part of man's fallen human nature that tends towards sinful desires. It is an active force to be dealt with in every person alive. Conquering that enemy is impossible unless they learn to walk in the Spirit.

Biblically speaking, walking in the Spirit is the only exercise that gives victory over the flesh. In fact, even if a person seems to win over sin by their own efforts, their victory can easily turn to pride or self-confidence, which is only another area of the flesh to conquer.

The Apostle Paul instructed the Galatian believers:

Galatians 5:16
I say then: Walk in the Spirit, and you shall not fulfill the lust of the flesh.

And he reveals that it is not demons who keep believers from doing what they want, but sinful flesh that stands in the way.

Verse 17
For the flesh lusts against the Spirit, and the Spirit against the flesh; and these are contrary to one another, so that you do not do the things that you wish.

Verse 24 continues:
And those who are Christ's have crucified the flesh with its passions and desires.

He does not say that those who have not crucified their flesh are not saved. He declares that those who are still controlled by other desires are not fully Christ's. They have given the flesh room to live and produce its works again.

The *"fruit of the Spirit"* comes as the result of having our life's roots (our thoughts and intentions) fully immersed into pleasing the Lord. The resulting fruit is seen in the spiritual form of loving expressions and gentle living. They come into our lives from walking in the Spirit.

The fruit of the Spirit produces action in human relationships and in commitment to God.

To be fully committed to walking in the Spirit, one must become fully convinced that nothing good will come from indulging the flesh. If a person becomes convinced of this, he will hate the flesh and do everything in his power to put it to death.

Every area of the flesh left alive develops more fleshly appetites. Sinful flesh does not remain passive or dormant. The flesh will grow and dominate if it is given time and space.

Giving time and space is offering thought and action to the flesh. The Apostle Paul called this *"sowing to the flesh."* And the man or woman who sows must expect a harvest from the seeds he or she sows. The Apostle made this quite clear:

Galatians 6:7-8
7 Do not be deceived, God is not mocked; for whatever a man sows, that he will also reap.
8 For he who sows to his flesh will of the flesh reap corruption, but he who sows to the Spirit will of the Spirit reap everlasting life.

He states that it isn't the devil creating the sin and it isn't God who condemns with corruption. Our own actions, indulgence, and tolerance of the flesh, sow the seeds of corruption that grow naturally of their own accord, but to Satan's great delight.

He reveals that the quality of life that is called *"everlasting life"* only comes to us as a result of *"sowing"* to the Spirit. And, that process brings to life the nature of the *new man* God has designed and prepared for each believer.

We must learn the process of *"putting off"* the old man, who operates according to the flesh, in order to *"put on the new man"* as explained in his Epistles.

Ephesians 4:21-24
21 If indeed you have heard Him and have been taught by Him, as the truth is in Jesus;
22 that you put off, concerning your former conduct, the old man which grows corrupt according to the deceitful lusts,
23 and be renewed in the spirit of your mind,
24 and that you put on the new man which was created according to God, in true righteousness and holiness.

It is not enough to put off the old alone. You must also *"be renewed in the spirit of your mind"*. Then you can put on the *"new man which was created according to God."*

This process was considered a primary life change principle among the early Christian Churches.

The principle is repeated in Paul's appeal to the Colossians regarding changing their conduct to be more pleasing to the Lord. Using lying as his place of entree he clarified the principle again:

Colossians 3:9-10
9 Do not lie to one another, since you have put off the old man with his deeds,
10 and have put on the new man who is renewed in knowledge according to the image of Him who created him,

Notice Paul's instructions to both these Churches:

* They were not just to patch up the old self. They were to completely put it off.

* They were not to change a little. They were to put on a new self, a new man created like its Creator.

He also tells us that the old man *"grows corrupt according to the deceitful lusts."*

The Apostle Peter reveals in *2 Peter 1:4* that by partaking of the *"divine nature"* we will *"escape"* the corruption that is *"in the world through lust."*

The order of renewal then is:

1. Put off the old self - through repentance.

Don't just turn away from the old. You must turn toward the new!

2. Be renewed in the spirit of your mind - by filling your heart and mind with God's Word.

3. Now you can put on the new self - through walking in the Spirit.

It is here that most Christians fall short. They endeavor to put off the old man without renewing their minds or putting on the new man. Even though they intend to be better, they never quite get the new self on. Instead, they try to doctor up the old self with religious practices in order to look acceptable to human eyes. But God doesn't accept an improved old man. He wants us to put on the new man.

Doctoring up the old man is futile, for it is impossible to overcome the flesh by fighting it according to the flesh.

The flesh is a spiritual force present within us and it needs to be overcome by spiritual means. Instead of trying to overcome our flesh in our own strength we must move into another realm of power and life.

Victory over this *"presence of sin in our members"* comes as we refuse to walk according to our fleshly appetites and learn to *"walk according to the Spirit."*

The primary goal then for each of us is to refuse any participation in our flesh with its desires, and learn to walk in the Spirit.

The Apostle Paul clearly says:

Galatians 5:16
I say then: Walk in the Spirit and you shall not fulfill the lust of the flesh.

You cannot walk in the Spirit with a carnal mind set. The ways we think, what we think about, and the attitudes we live by, hinder our ability to even perceive our own carnality.

Therefore we must acknowledge that the renewing of our minds is an essential ingredient in the process. Paul continued:

Romans 8:5-8
For those who live according to the flesh set their minds on the things of the flesh, but those who live according to the Spirit, the things of the Spirit.
6 For to be carnally minded is death, but to be spiritually minded is life and peace.
7 Because the carnal mind is enmity against God; for it is not subject to the law of God, nor indeed can be.
8 So then, those who are in the flesh cannot please God.

Whether a professing Christian, or a committed agnostic, the flesh will operate in as much territory as it is given. Believers are not excluded. Flesh still creates its corruption wherever it finds an unrepentant or unsubmitted area of life to grow in.

Romans 8:12-14
Therefore, brethren, we are debtors—not to the flesh, to live according to the flesh.
13 For if you live according to the flesh you will die; but if by the Spirit you put to death the deeds of the body, you will live.
14 For as many as are led by the Spirit of God, these are sons of God.

The ramifications of not walking in the Spirit are deadness of spirit and death to destiny.

Walking in the Spirit is not an option for the believer. It is the only way to freedom and fulfillment.

The Eagle is Flying

Isaiah 40:28-31

28 *Have you not known?*
Have you not heard?
The everlasting God, the Lord,
The creator of the ends of the earth,
Neither faints nor is weary.
His understanding is unsearchable.
29 *He gives power to the weak,*
And to those who have no might He increases strength.
30 *Even the youths shall faint and be weary,*
And the young men shall utterly fall.
31 *But those who wait on the Lord*
Shall renew their strength;
They shall mount up with wings like eagles,
They shall run and not be weary.
They shall walk and not faint.

The Prophet Isaiah wrote in powerfully colorful language, and with significant imagery, about the possibilities of those who will walk in the power of the Holy Spirit. Using the eagle as his example, he declares that the *"strength"* which God will give to us will surpass the strength of youth. And then He reveals that it is given to those who *"wait on the Lord"*.

The eagle has always been seen as a special bird. The early fathers of the United States of America adopted the eagle as the symbol of the nation. Before that, the native people of America chose eagle feathers to decorate their chiefs and convey honor and authority upon them.

The prophet Isaiah could not have known what we know today about the eagle.

Since man has developed flight as a means of travel and the airplane has come into our culture, eagles have been observed at tremendous heights, flying almost effortlessly, using the wind and the different currents of the wind to soar above the earth.

It is extremely significant that the Holy Spirit would give this clear and dynamic picture of the possibilities for those who will *"wait on the Lord."*

Eagles are able to walk on the ground. They have legs and feet that support and propel them when they are on the ground. However, even though they are able to walk and even run, an eagle on the ground is awkward and lacking in grace in comparison to an eagle in flight.

This is a powerful picture of the believer who never learns to abandon the walk of the flesh and move into the power of the Holy Spirit.

The eagle's body is made to walk on the earth and also to soar in the clouds. However, it only uses its walking ability occasionally. An eagle never decides to live complacently on the ground. Even his roosting and nesting places are found in the highest places of his earthly dwelling.

The imagery grows very similar to the Christian believer when we consider the difficulty of the eagle's flight. It takes more energy to take flight than it takes to keep flying. And the higher it flies, the more it can glide, and the longer it can stay aloft.

For an eagle to take flight he must use his legs to jump into the air so that his great wings can take over. Then his legs and talons are folded close to his body so that they will not disturb his flying.

His wings are powered by great muscles that have very little use when he walks on the ground. They are shaped in such a way that their movement propels him forward and upward at the same time. It is then that his tail feathers become part of his guidance and support system. When in flight, each part of his body cooperates in majestic harmony to enable him to soar above the earth with grace and beauty.

Once he learns to fly he never returns to the earth except for food and rest, because he loves to fly.

While meditating on the need to write this book I felt the Holy Spirit lead me to use the airplane as an example. However, the airplane is not a biblical figure, so I was unsure and refrained for some time. Then it came to me that most of the principles of aerodynamics that are built so beautifully into the eagle are the same principles that an airplane is built upon. Yet because it is mechanical and not a living thing, the components are separated from each other more clearly than the body of an eagle.

An airplane is built so that it is aerodynamic. That is, it is friendly to the air, and uses the air for its "lift". The curvature of its wings is designed to cause the air to pass quicker on the top side of the wing thus creating a vacuum that "lifts" the plane into the air.

The problem is that the plane has to be moving forward at enough speed to create this lift dynamic. Hence the propeller or jet propulsion engine that creates the forward speed.

Once the plane is moving fast enough on the ground, the plane is moved into flight by slight changes in the wings "flaps". It is then, when the plane is in the air that it also will fold up its wheels and become guided by the subtle changes in its wings, its tail flaps, and its rudder.

As soon as it is in the air and gains the appropriate speed the pilot will make minor adjustments to these several components so that the least resistance to flight is maintained. This is what is called "trimming" the plane so that even the shape of the vessel helps it fly.

This is a powerful example of how we are *"wonderfully and fearfully made"* to live and walk in the realm of the Holy Spirit rather than be dominated by the forces of the sinful flesh.

When we are born again, we take on the likeness of our Heavenly Father. He places a measure of His own Spirit in us that causes us to desire heavenly things.

He is not like us. He wants us to be more like Him. And one of His attributes is revealed in Verse 28.

Isaiah 40:28

Have you not known?
Have you not heard?
The everlasting God, the Lord,
The creator of the ends of the earth,
Neither faints nor is weary.

You and I are subjected to energy drains. We know what it is to get tired, and weary. As we get older, weariness becomes an even greater factor. But the Lord does not get weary.

Verse 29

He gives power to the weak,
And to those who have no might He increases strength.

Spiritual strength is one of the major issues the Lord deals with. He has given us a way to enter and live in the realm of His own power. Not yet in total fullness, but enough power so that we can be what He designed us to be, and accomplish what we are called to do.

The Lord *"gives power to the weak, and to those who have no might He increases strength."* This is important to know.

Verses 30-31

30 Even the youths shall faint and be weary,
And the young men shall utterly fall.
31 But those who wait on the Lord
Shall renew their strength;
They shall mount up with wings like eagles,
They shall run and not be weary.

They shall walk and not faint.

Isaiah saw through the inspiration of the Holy Spirit that a certain relationship with the Lord would give extra strength to His people that would enable them to *"mount up with wings like eagles."*

This is the allegorical picture of those who learn to walk in the power of the Holy Spirit and refuse to be bound by their ties to earthly things. It was given to us so that we would not remain content with life in the flesh.

Waiting on the Lord

Waiting on the Lord is a key element to all of this. Yet few really seem to understand this principle enough to obey it consistently.

To "wait" is translated from the word *"qavah"* in the Hebrew text of the Old Testament. According to the Strong's Hebrew and Chaldee Dictionary it means to *bind* together (perh. by *twisting*) i.e. *collect;* (fig.) to *expect:-* gather (together), look, patiently, tarry, wait (for, on, upon). It is an amazing word that describes powerfully the spiritual exercise of waiting on the Lord.

The word is used in other places as *"wait for the Lord"*. This seems to be the understanding of most Christians, for they seem to be inactive while they wait for God to do something for them.

However, when we join the word "on" or "upon", as the King James and the New King James versions do, we understand it as taking the place of a servant of the Lord.

Much like a waiter in a restaurant waits on or upon his customers, the servant position of waiting on the Lord is the place of release for this dynamic strength Isaiah speaks of.

The Psalms also speak of this kind of waiting:

Psalm 27:14

Wait on the Lord;
Be of good courage,
And He shall strengthen your heart;
Wait, I say, on the Lord.

The Apostle Paul also wrote of the availability of greater measures of strength for the believers. In his epistle to the Ephesians he wrote:

Ephesians 6:10
Finally, my brethren, be strong in the Lord and in the power of His might.

Like the flight of the eagle, there is power to soar in the things of God for those who wait on Him.

Chapter 2
Becoming Servants

Probably the biggest hindrance to walking in the Spirit is the self-serving mind set we carry from childhood. It is the mindset that our own desires and our own needs are preeminent above every one and everything else.

It is a fact that many Christians today accept the Lord as Savior thinking that He will serve their own personal needs and purposes. Therefore Christian service is not something they easily move into. However, as long as a person hangs onto the mind set of their own needs first, they will have difficulty ever having a continued intimate relationship with Jesus, because our new life is really not about us.

My life is not really about me, and your life is not about you. Our lives are about Him. And, they are about how they can be given to bless and increase others.

Jesus made this very clear to His Disciples:

Luke17:33
"Whoever seeks to save his life will lose it, and whoever loses his life will preserve it."

Paul explained the principle to the Galatians. It must be our starting point. He wrote:

Galatians 5:13-14
13 For you, brethren, have been called to liberty; only do not use liberty as an opportunity for the flesh, but through love serve one another.
14 For all the law is fulfilled in one word, even in this: "You shall love your neighbor as yourself."

Let's break this down:

"For you, brethren:" He is not talking about a special group, like the ministry team, or the Church Council. He is talking to "the brethren." These are all those who have been born again and brought into the family of God.

"have been called to liberty:" All of us have been called by God out of the bondage to self and sin. Jesus' own victory on the cross and in His resurrection was for our *"liberty"*.

"only do not use liberty as an opportunity for the flesh:" Being set free from all the penalties of sin and its power over us has not been given so that we can return again to their service and lifestyle. It is the flesh that got us into this mess in the first place. We must not hang on to the spiritual foundation of selfishness that enabled the flesh to dominate us in the first place. We need to move away from selfishness and into the calling of God.

Remember, the flesh is that part of our nature that puts itself first. Serving one's self is the primary motivation that attracts all the other lusts and desires, and opens the door for Satan to manipulate and govern our lives.

If you still serve yourself, you are using your liberty from sin in the wrong way.

"but through love serve one another:" Humble servanthood to God, and then to each other, creates the spiritual foundation for the Holy Spirit to work and build upon.

The Holy Spirit will not guide and lead the person who lives for himself.

You must pull away from the selfishness of your old man. This is how you put him to death. You refuse to allow him to rule your life. This is the foundational decision of life in the Spirit.

The old man is self-directed, self-centered and selfish. As a result it is not serving, not caring, and not sensitive to other people's needs.

The mind of Christ is servant centered. It is God serving, people loving, and Holy Spirit sensitive. Faithful servanthood becomes the mind-set and objective of all those who truly walk in the Spirit.

The mind of Christ

The mind of Christ is not the ability of knowing all the thoughts of others as if we were clairvoyant. It is not *"word of knowledge,"* or being "prophetic".

The Apostle Paul coined this phrase by using Jesus' own life purpose and servant attitude as the example for us to seek and follow:

Philippians 2:1-11
1 Therefore if there is any consolation in Christ, if any comfort of love, if any fellowship of the Spirit, if any affection and mercy,
2 fulfill my joy by being like-minded, having the same love, being of one accord, of one mind.
3 Let nothing be done through selfish ambition or conceit, but in lowliness of mind let each esteem others better than himself.
4 Let each of you look out not only for his own interests, but also for the interests of others.
5 Let this mind be in you which was also in Christ Jesus,
6 who, being in the form of God, did not consider it robbery to be equal with God,
7 but made Himself of no reputation, taking the form of a bondservant, and coming in the likeness of men.
8 And being found in appearance as a man, He humbled Himself and became obedient to the point of death, even the death of the cross.
9 Therefore God also has highly exalted Him and given Him the name which is above every name,
10 that at the name of Jesus every knee should bow, of those in heaven, and of those on earth, and of those under the earth,

11 and that every tongue should confess that Jesus Christ is Lord, to the glory of God the Father.

“The mind of Jesus” was not self directed, self exalting, self seeking, or selfish. He humbled himself and became a servant. He chose to become the servant of God the Father, and the Father sent Him to serve mankind on His behalf.

That is precisely why we have been saved from sin’s power. It is so that we also can be free to serve God, and He commands us to love and serve each other.

If you do not become a servant to God and His people you can not walk in the Spirit. Selfishness is in itself opposed to being led of the Holy Spirit, for it is the Holy Spirit that equips and fills us for servanthood.

Questions to ponder:

Who do you serve?

Who are the people God has given you to serve?

Are you serving them on God’s behalf?

Do you serve in God’s Church? How?

Chapter 3
Connecting

When we decide to serve we become aware of our need to receive more strength and grace than ever before. There are many who try to serve in their own strength and find themselves becoming exhausted and disillusioned. They easily become discouraged and return to their old ways, justifying themselves by the excuse, "I tried and just couldn't do it". So we must seek the power and anointing of God so that our service may be effective.

Serving people is not easy. However, it can be much easier than we think if we do it in the right way and for the right reasons.

The life journey of service is meant to provide help for those in need, but also an incentive to draw us closer to God through partnering with Him in redemptive purposes. We know Him best when we come to Him and take on His yoke. However, we will wear out and become weary and heavy laden if we try to carry the yoke of service in our own power.

The abiding relationship

Psalm 91:1

> *He who dwells in the secret place of the Most High*
> *Shall abide under the shadow of the Almighty.*

When He began His public ministry, Jesus taught His Disciples about a new way of living He called "the Kingdom of God". He continued to preach John the Baptist's message regarding repentance, but added new purposes to it.

Repentance is a "turning from". But to complete the equation we must also "turn to" something new or we will automatically return to our old ways.

Communicating the elements of the Kingdom of God to disciples that already had their own ideas and concepts was extremely difficult. They understood repentance as turning from sinful actions. Jesus was teaching a repentance that reached beyond surface actions and into the heart, soul, and mind. Each Disciple's emotional focus, life purposes and legalistic concepts, were standing in the way of understanding the Kingdom of God. So Jesus used new and different language to communicate His message. He spoke in parables, in word pictures, and most powerfully through what we call "modeling" the Kingdom, His own life example.

One of the most powerful times of communication was the word picture he painted of the vine and its' branches found in the Gospel of John.

It was given at the Last Supper.

The twelve Disciples were gathered around Him in close intimacy. He was speaking with close eye contact and great feeling and emotion.

He had just asked them to trust in Him as they had trusted the Father. Then He told them that He must go away from them, and yet somehow would still be with them. Let's break into the conversation:

John 14:15-18
"If you love Me, keep My commandments.
16 "And I will pray the Father, and He will give you another Helper, that He may abide with you forever—
17 "the Spirit of truth, whom the world cannot receive, because it neither sees Him nor knows Him; but you know Him, for He dwells with you and will be in you.
18 "I will not leave you orphans; I will come to you.

Today, because we are able to see in hindsight, we understand that Jesus was promising to come to them through the Holy Spirit. Then, He continued speaking to them in picture form about the necessity of living constantly connected to Him through the power and presence of the Spirit.

Jesus called this kind of living, *"Abiding in Me"*

John 15:4-5
4 "Abide in Me, and I in you. As the branch cannot bear fruit of itself, unless it abides in the vine, neither can you, unless you abide in Me.
5 I am the vine, you are the branches. He who abides in Me, and I in him, bears much fruit; for without Me you can do nothing."

This powerful word picture explains so dramatically, and beautifully, what living in the Spirit is.

Personal testimony

When I was just a boy, growing up in our Christian family, my mother, who was a very practical and nurturing woman, was also my Sunday School teacher.

Sometimes on Saturday evenings she would share with me what she was going to teach the next morning. And sometimes she would involve me in her lessons as the class example.

On one of those times, as she prepared her lesson for the next morning, she asked me to help her make her presentation. I agreed to do so. So just before leaving for Sunday school the next morning, she called me and asked me to go into the garden in the back yard and cut off some branches from our grape vine.

I was happy to do so and brought them to her very carefully, to try and keep them from losing their leaves or from wilting. She took them from me and then put them in water and we headed for Sunday school. I was excited and very curious to find out what she was going to do with the grape branches in the class.

After talking about vines and sharing the Scripture text regarding the Vine and His branches, she took the branches I had cut for her and held them up in front of us. She handed them out to each child in the class. Then she asked us if we thought these branches had any chance of bearing grapes now that they were cut off of the vine.

After a few moments of quiet, she asked us if there was any chance that they would even live very long.

When we quietly responded "no" to both questions, she read again Jesus' words to His Disciples on that special occasion before He died for them.

After we discussed the life process that kept the branches alive, she asked us if we thought any of us could be fruitful unto God if we kept disconnecting from Jesus' presence. We realized that we couldn't even live without Him.

I never forgot that lesson. It has become part of my concept of living in the Spirit.

The picture of the vine and the branches explains how fruitfulness comes into our lives. For, the life of each branch is found in the sap that flows from the root through the vine and into the branches to produce life and fruitfulness. Fruit is the result of that life flow.

A branch can only bear fruit if it remains connected deeply and constantly to the vine. Any disconnection cuts off the flow of the life giving sap that flows through the branch to each leaf and produces the fruit.

The "abiding in the vine" process is what living continually in the Spirit is all about.

Just as the vine begins to wither the moment it becomes disconnected from its life source, so we begin to wither spiritually any time we become disconnected from our life source, The Holy Spirit!

Some believers practice a life style of "connect-disconnect-reconnect" and wonder why they feel withered and fruitless. In fact, those who practice this style of living usually don't even consider bearing fruit.

They are barely able to stay alive.

Jesus warned us that if we disconnect from His presence, we cannot bear fruit, instead we will wither.

How many spiritually withered Christians do we see in our times? They seem to be good people. They try to live good lives. But they are spiritually withered and fruitless. Most of the time fruitlessness is not a matter of the actions of sinning, but the result of the carnal mind set that tells them they don't need to be deeply attached and continually connected to Jesus through the Holy Spirit.

Prayer is our principle means of connecting

The Bibles teaches that the primary gateway to walking in the Spirit is prayer. Praying according to the Spirit is the only way to remain "plugged in" to Jesus.

Prayer is one of the most wonderful gifts God has given to man. By placing our minds on God and expressing our thinking and desires in words to Him, He draws near and accepts those words and thoughts as valid relationship with Him. God literally listens to our prayers!

Prayer is made up of our human words brought to God in the form of conversation and communion.

To fully understand prayer, we must grasp what the Bible teaches about our words and communication process.

Words can have great spiritual power. All of our words are important, because they are expressions of our heart's thinking. They literally express and reveal our inner person.

Let's look at the power of our words from a Scriptural perspective first.

Proverbs 18:21

Death and life are in the power of the tongue,
And those who love it will eat its fruit.

Proverbs 12:13-14

13 The wicked is ensnared by the transgression of his lips,
But the righteous will come through trouble.
14 A man will be satisfied with good by the fruit of his mouth.

Proverbs 13:3

He who guards his mouth preserves his life,
But he who opens wide his lips shall have destruction.

Proverbs 14:3

In the mouth of a fool is a rod of pride.
But the lips of the wise will preserve them.

Proverbs 18:7

A fool's mouth is his destruction,
And his lips are the snare of his soul.

Jesus emphasized the importance of each person's words:

Matthew 12:36-37
36 "But I say to you that for every idle word men may speak, they will give account of it in the day of judgment.
37 "For by your words you will be justified, and by your words you will be condemned."

The Apostle Paul taught us that it is by confessing with our mouths that we are saved.

Romans 10:10
For with the heart one believes unto righteousness, and with the mouth confession is made unto salvation.

The Apostle James (in *James 3 verses 3-4*) tells us that our tongues can set our course in life just like a bit in its mouth steers a horse, and a rudder steers a ship.

What you say tends to steer you and set your future direction.

James also taught us that our tongues can be set on fire from hell itself.

James 3:6
And the tongue is a fire, a world of iniquity. The tongue is so set among our members that it defiles the whole body, and sets on fire the course of nature; and it is set on fire by hell.

Because of this, James tells us that we must *"bridle our tongues"* in order to live godly lives.

James 1:26
If anyone among you thinks he is religious, and does not bridle his tongue but deceives his own heart, this one's religion is useless.

We *"bridle"* our tongues by controlling our speech. Our tongues are bridled when we refuse to allow our flesh to work through our speech, but instead, we direct our tongues to another kind of conversation, we direct them to spiritual, life giving conversation.

The secret of redirecting our members

The secret of victory over sins' dominion in our flesh is to appropriate Christ's victory over sin, and refuse to let it reign in any of the members of our bodies. As important as each member of our bodies are, it is especially important to refuse to let sin rule our tongues and our speech habits.

Listen again to the Apostle Paul's exhortations to the Roman believers:

Romans 6:12-13
12 Therefore do not let sin reign in your mortal body, that you should

obey it in its lusts.
13 And do not present your members as instruments of unrighteousness to sin, but present yourselves to God as being alive from the dead, and your members as instruments of righteousness to God.

The way to impede the reign of sin in our lives is by refusing to allow our members to be used any longer for unrighteous purposes. Instead, they should be offered to God as instruments of righteousness.

Yielding our tongues to God

Our tongues can be used as a constant source of relationship with God. We can now offer them to Him through prayer, and they can be the instruments of prayer that He intended. They can keep us in constant open relationship to the Spirit.

If we give them to prayer continually, then they will not be used as instruments of evil! They can set holy fires in us instead of the unholy fires of conflict and lust.

Prayer is the gateway to the Holy Spirit, for prayer connects us to God.

A person will learn to walk in the Spirit as he or she learns to pray earnestly and fervently.

In Paul's Epistle to the Ephesians, he commands them to put on God's strength and His armor. He reveals that this can only be accomplished as we learn to pray effectively. Listen closely as we enter the conversation at *Verse 17*:

Ephesians 6:17-18
17 And take the helmet of salvation, and the sword of the Spirit, which is the word of God;
18 praying always with all prayer and supplication in the Spirit, being watchful to this end with all perseverance and supplication for all the saints—

You learn to walk in the Spirit by first learning to pray in the Spirit.

There really is no other way. Remember, prayer is not man's invention. Prayer is God's own gift to mankind that enables us to relate to Him.

Prayer is my spirit's own language. It enables limited human beings to actually connect through their spirits to God's Spirit in life giving communion.

Praying in the Spirit in the context of Paul's exhortations to the Ephesians, is much more than the religious exercise of speaking prayerful words to a distant being. Praying in the Spirit is the kind of prayer God has given the believer who has been baptized into Christ through the Spirit. Prayer is enhanced and amplified through the Baptism of the Holy Spirit.

Prayer in the Spirit connects people, whose spirits have been made alive and sensitive, to the Holy Spirit, who is the primary agent of God's presence. This connection of "prayer in the Spirit" is the channel from which God can speak to us, and the way His very Life can flow into us. Prayer is the spiritual connection of communication.

Prayer in the Spirit offers more than just me talking to God. It allows prayer to become God's means of conversing and manifesting His life to me.

Questions to ponder:

1. Do you remain constantly connected to Jesus? Or do you only visit with Him on occasions?

2. Do you still hold your own needs as preeminent? Or are you convinced that serving others is your life's goal and privilege?

3. Do you pray so that you can live in constant relationship with God?

Or do you pray to get what you want from God?

4. Do you abide in the vine? Or do you live much of the time disconnected from Him?

Chapter 4
All kinds of Prayers - I

Ephesians 6:18 NIV
And pray in the Spirit on all occasions with all kinds of prayers and requests. With this in mind, be alert and always keep on praying for all the saints.

Let's explore some powerful ways of praying in the Spirit that are written in the Bible yet are not commonly understood.

Remember that all prayer teachings must be based on the foundation of what Jesus taught His disciples.

The prayer of declaration

The "declaring prayer" gets its name from Jesus' personal teachings to His Disciples regarding prayer.

The occasion took place during Jesus' last few days in Jerusalem before His crucifixion. He and the Disciples were staying outside the city and then walking back into the city for the ministry times in the Temple area. On one of those walks Jesus approached a fig tree, looking for fruit on it. When it had none, He spoke to the tree!

Mark 11:12-14
12 Now the next day, when they had come out from Bethany He was hungry.
13 And seeing from afar a fig tree having leaves. He went to see if perhaps He would find something on it. When He came to it, He found nothing but leaves, for it was not the season for figs.
14 In response Jesus said to it, "Let no one eat fruit from you ever again." And His disciples heard it.

Then the writer tells us what happened the next day:

Verses 20-24
20 Now in the morning, as they passed by, they saw the fig tree dried up from the roots.
21 And Peter, remembering, said to Him, "Rabbi, look! The fig tree which You cursed has withered away."
22 So Jesus answered and said to them. "Have faith in God.
23 "For assuredly, I say to you, whoever says to this mountain, 'Be removed and be cast into the sea, and does not doubt in his heart, but believes that those things he says will be done, he will have whatever he says.
24 Therefore I say to you, whatever things you ask when you pray, believe that you receive them, and you will have them.

Jesus had been observed "declaring in prayer". His explanation shows that this is in fact a valid form of prayer.

Notice that Peter mistakenly called this "cursing"!

We see the "declaring prayer" being taught for the first time in the beginning of Jesus' ministry to the Disciples in the Sermon on the Mount, given near the Sea of Galilee.

First He taught them how not to pray!

Matthew 6:5-8
5 "And when you pray, you shall not be like the hypocrites. For they love to pray standing in the synagogues and on the corners of the streets, that they may be seen by men. Assuredly, I say to you, they have their reward.
6 "But you, when you pray, go into your room, and when you have shut your door, pray to your Father who is in the secret place; and your Father who sees in secret will reward you openly.
7 "And when you pray, do not use vain repetitions as the heathen do. For they think that they will be heard for their many words.
8 "Therefore do not be like them. For your Father knows the things

you have need of before you ask Him.

The first example is the prayer of the hypocrite. They love to pray in a way that men can see them and be impressed at their spirituality.

Jesus said that the foundation of prayer is to be alone, intimate and honest with God. Our motives must be purely to draw near to Him, and to please Him.

He commanded specifically:

Verse 6
But you, when you pray, go into your room, and when you have shut your door, pray to your Father who is in the secret place; and your Father who sees in secret will reward you openly.

Find a place you can be alone and shut everyone but God out of it. Then, pray to your Father. The secret prayer life is what pleases God.

The second example is the example of the heathen.

Verses 7-8
7 "And when you pray, do not use vain repetitions as the heathen do. For they think that they will be heard for their many words.
8 "Therefore do not be like them. For your Father knows the things you have need of before you ask Him.

The heathen culture felt that communication with the gods had to be rigorous and articulate, mystical and magical. Much emphasis was put on the amount of time and words put into their prayers.

The same is true of many Christians today. They think that prayer quality is measured in their ability to articulate, and by the amount of time spent.

Jesus said that we should not be like them.

Instead, He gave us specific instructions about what we should pray about, and the method of prayer to use in order to draw near to the Father and please Him. It is called the Lord's Prayer, but should be more accurately called the Disciple's prayer agenda. For much of this agenda could not be His prayer. (He had no sin and no need of forgiveness.)

Let's look closely at it together:

Matthew 6:9-13
9 In this manner, therefore, pray:

Our Father in heaven,
Hallowed be Your name.
10 Your kingdom come.
Your will be done
On earth as it is in heaven.
11 Give us this day our daily bread.
12 And forgive us our debts,
As we forgive our debtors.
13 And do not lead us into temptation,
But deliver us from the evil one.
For Yours is the kingdom, and the
Power, and the glory forever. Amen.

The Sermon on the Mount was not the only recorded occasion that Jesus gave this particular instruction. The same prayer format is found again at a later date. The occasion took place on the Mount of Olives near Jerusalem.

Luke 11:1-4
1 Now it came to pass, as He was praying in a certain place, when he
ceased, that one of His disciples said to Him, "Lord teach us to pray,
as John also taught his disciples."
2 So he said to them, "When you pray, say:

Our Father in heaven.
Hallowed be Your name.
Your kingdom come.
Your will be done
On earth as it is in heaven.
3 *Give us day by day our daily bread.*
4 *And forgive us our sins,*
For we also forgive everyone who
is indebted to us.
And do not lead us into temptation,
But deliver us from the evil one."

The disciples' request shows that His initial instructions had not been put into practice. The disciples were observing Jesus in prayer but not enjoying the same prayer experience.

His answer to their need was to take them back to the basic prayer agenda He had given them at the beginning.

The repetition shows us its importance. It is the foundation of all our prayers of understanding.

Remember, the Apostle Paul had written:

1 Corinthians 14:15
"I will pray with the spirit, and I will also pray with the understanding."

So, as we look at the prayers of understanding, we need to "understand" the "declaring prayer" that Jesus taught us. In both instances of the Lord's Prayer, there is a mixture of statements directed toward spiritual obstacles, and prayers of petition to the Lord.

First the Father is addressed plainly:

"Our Father in heaven."

It is extremely important to be certain that we address specifically who we are praying to.

Then we find the first “declaring prayer”.

“Hallowed be Your name.”

Here we are not asking The Father to *“hallow”* His own Name. We are instead speaking spiritually to our own course and purpose in life. We are “declaring” what needs to be done. Yet this “declaration” is done in the context of praying in the very presence of God.

Remember what the Apostle James taught us:

James 3:3-4
3 Indeed, we put bits in horses’ mouths that they may obey us, and we turn their whole body.
4 Look also at ships: although they are so large and are driven by fierce winds, they are turned by a very small rudder wherever the pilot desires.

The context here is being steered, setting our course and direction in life. The very next verse starts with the words - *“Even so the tongue...”*

It is clear that God is revealing again that our own life’s direction can be steered by what we “say” or “declare” in prayer.

To say *“Hallowed be Your name,”* is to speak new purpose and direction to our own hearts.

* It confronts our natural desire to have our own names exalted, and lifts His name above all things.

* It is the course setting statement that brings our personal agendas under His agenda.

* It sets and confirms my desire to exalt His name in everything I do and say.

It is a powerful form of prayer!

The same is true with each of the next two powerful “declarations of prayer.”

"Your kingdom come,
Your will be done on earth as it is in heaven."

The meaning of these "prayer declarations" is significant.

The word *"kingdom"* comes from the Greek work "basilea", meaning "rulership", or "realm of rulership." When we say, (as the original does) "Come your Kingdom!" we are speaking our own course of direction. We are moving against the "mountain" of self-rule. And we are speaking God's form of rulership into our daily living.

The prayer statement "*Your will be done*" does the same thing, except that it goes into what we actually seek to accomplish, as well as what our attitudes should be while we accomplish it. "*Your will be done on earth as it is done in heaven."*

When this prayer is spoken by those with understanding, it cries out before God for the "will of God to be done" in their own lives, with the same joy, enthusiasm, and willingness that all the angels of heaven manifest when doing God's holy bidding.

By "speaking spiritual direction" as normal prayer relationship, we become comfortable with this dimension of prayer. As we learn its value and become aware of the flow of the Spirit in it, we will find the Holy Spirit leading us to "speak" to other "mountains" and obstacles in our own lives, and in those we serve and minister to.

Remember: This kind of speaking and declaring must remain within the parameters of spiritual authority and the purpose of edification. It must never be used to "control", or to manipulate another person's decision. It must never speak an invitation of evil or trouble on another person. We must speak *"blessing"* and not *"cursing."*

The "prayer of declaration" is very important to learn and include in our prayer experience, because walking in the Spirit is totally dependent upon being "ruled" by the Spirit, and being actively involved in "doing" the will of God.

The "prayer of declaration" assails the "mountains" of self-direction and selfishness, and sets our own course into alignment with the Holy Spirit's purposes.

Asking Prayer

Another kind of prayer is the "asking prayer". It is also seen in Jesus' teachings in the Lord's Prayer.

After we have established our purpose and direction through the "prayer of declaration", we are taught to bring our needs before God in "supplication."

Supplication is "humble entreaty" before God. (Webster's Dictionary)

To supplicate is to ask for something in the correct way.

Ephesians 6:18
- praying always with all prayer and supplication in the Spirit, being watchful to this end with all perseverance and supplication for all the saints.

Supplication is the asking prayer of understanding. Yet, it is still being guided by the Holy Spirit. It is prayer immersed in the Spirit.

Supplication is to be addressed toward our own and other peoples needs as well. Jesus taught us to ask:

"Give us this day our daily bread"

We find a number of issues in this short supplication.

Jesus is revealing to us how to receive God's provision. Many live below their possibilities because they do not understand this form of prayer, or God's desire to provide.

Asking prayer brings us into:

* Agreement with God that our natural needs are supplied through His provision.

* Agreement that these needs should be a daily provision instead of a storing up of wealth.

* Agreement that we need this day's bread today.

Daily Bread is a subject of major importance. It includes many forms of provision, both natural and spiritual. It is not limited to our natural need for food at all.

Natural bread

Natural "bread" includes all that we need in the way of human provision. It is God's will that we learn to pray for it. It is part of walking in the Spirit.

Prayer for bread teaches us to receive correctly. For when we understand that even our daily food provision comes from God, we treat it all differently.

We become "stewards" rather than "owners" of our possessions.

We become open and ready to share with others as the Spirit leads.

We become givers, as God leads, because we understand that He is our provider and that our resources are not limited. Therefore we have no fear of tomorrow, even though we cannot see tomorrow's provision with our natural eyes.

Spiritual bread

John 6:51

I am the living bread which came down from heaven. If anyone eats of this bread, he will live forever, and the bread that I shall give is My flesh, which I shall give for the life of the world.

Jesus called Himself the Bread from heaven.

Spiritual provision comes from prayer as well. In the same way that manna was given daily to the children of Israel in the wilderness experience, Jesus revealed that there is a daily impartation of Himself available to us from His Word and His Presence. By asking for *"daily bread"* with understanding, we become expectant seekers and receivers of spiritual bread too.

We miss many precious spiritual gifts by not being expectant. Just as manna in the wilderness was found as they looked for it, even so spiritual bread is also found as we walk in the Spirit, watching for it.

We need every day's supply of both natural and spiritual provision.

We are encouraged to ask for them confidently.

Questions to ponder:

1. Do you pray after the model Jesus gave us in the Lord's prayer?

2. Do you seek spiritual bread daily as you do natural bread?

3. Is your prayer life primarily a means of receiving from God, or is it mostly your means of connection and relationship with Him?

4. Does your prayer life demonstrate that you are God's servant, or that you are seeking Him to serve you?

Chapter 5
All kinds of Prayer - II

Forgiveness

The next supplication is extremely important.

"Forgive us our debts,
As we forgive our debtors."

To forgive means: to excuse, to pardon, to remit or cancel a debt. (Webster's Dictionary)

The word "debts" explains the scope of what we are to ask forgiveness for. The word "debts" includes more than what we have done, it includes the things we have not done that we should have, and those things we have not become that God asks of us. A debt is what we owe God and each other.

We are instructed to ask that God would treat our *"debts"* with His forgiveness, as we do the same with those we are in relationship with.

In doing this we set up the foundation for Spirit led relationships. And, we establish the groundwork for the way we are to respond to other people's actions and attitudes.

It all begins and ends with forgiveness.

* Forgiveness is not trust. But it opens the way for trust to be established.

* Forgiveness is not restoration. But it opens the way for restoration to begin.

When you forgive, you eliminate the offense as a barrier to relationship. Trust may still have to be reestablished, and restoration may have to be worked out, but the foundation has been laid for these to happen.

The reason that Jesus included forgiveness in our daily prayer agenda is that it is so very important. The way to live continually in God's forgiveness is by continually giving forgiveness. You cannot walk in the Spirit while holding unforgiveness in your heart.

When we pray for forgiveness we become conscious of how God forgives, and how we receive it as a gracious gift from Him. We become aware of our need to be constantly forgiving on the same basis of grace.

The final petition:

And do not lead us into temptation,
But deliver us from the evil one.

This supplication is meant to secure deliverance through relationship with God rather than through the process of temptation and failure. It carries with it the understanding that God will *"lead us into temptation"*, especially if we allow sinful desires to grow in us and are not delivered through the prayer process.

One of temptation's main purposes is to reveal the hidden desires of sin.

Jesus was led into the wilderness to be tempted of the Devil. He overcame in this most fierce temptation by yielding completely to the will of the Father and by speaking the Word of God in complete obedience.

God does not tempt us. However, He does lead us into situations of temptation that will reveal our heart's true condition. He does this: so that we can strengthen our desire for complete obedience; and deal with sin in its seed form of desire before it grows up and produces sinful actions; and so that we can learn to face our humanity and its weaknesses with God's own Word as our spiritual sword of defense.

James 1:12-15

12 Blessed is the man who endures temptation; for when he has been approved, he will receive the crown of life which the Lord has promised to those who love Him.
13 Let no one say when he is tempted, "I am tempted by God", for God cannot be tempted by evil, nor does He Himself tempt anyone.
14 But each one is tempted when he is drawn away by his own desires and enticed.
15 Then, when desire has conceived, it gives birth to sin; and sin, when it is full-grown, brings forth death.

The principle of conception and birthing of sin

The Apostle James reveals how sin develops through the "seed" of desire.

The desire is planted and cultivated in our hearts. Then it is conceived into our being by our consent or toleration.

Conception enables the sin to live and grow in our hearts in the form of lust.

Lust is the change from natural, controllable desire, to controlling desire. It comes into our hearts in seed form and when given room, will grow into domination. After conception, the person becomes "pregnant" with sin. The seed of desire grows until it controls thoughts and then actions.

The incubation of lust prepares our heart and mind for subsequent sinful action. Sinful action breaks fellowship with God and brings death into our lives.

God's mercy causes Him to intervene in this process by leading us through situations that will reveal our hearts true desires. He does not tempt us. He leads us in paths of righteousness, but if we allow the flesh to create desires that will lead us into sin, He will allow temptation to cross that pathway.

Temptation gives us the chance to recognize, confront, and cleanse the sinfulness of evil desire before it produces sinful actions and the damage to our intimacy with God.

However, God would rather reveal and remove evil desires through the prayer process than through the temptation process. So we are taught to pray: *"lead us not into temptation but deliver us from the evil one."*

He uses the term "*evil one*" so that we will fully understand that when we yield ourselves servants to sin, we become servants to the "*one*" who orchestrates sin behind the scenes, Satan.

Praise prayer - the confession of God's greatness

Jesus finishes the prayer agenda by a statement of truth and praise:

"For Yours is the kingdom, and the power, and the glory, forever. Amen"

Here we find the affirmation of His power to accomplish all that we have asked and believed for. This is "praise prayer". It is the expression of full agreement with who God is; His awesome ability; and His eternal presence. Praise Prayer is a form of prayer Jesus called "words that justify" us.

It is the praise-prayer of encouragement and victory to our own selves.

Praise prayer not only sets our course in believing, but helps us remember that He is able and willing to do all these things we have brought before Him.

The Apostle Paul wrote:

Ephesians 3:20-21
20 Now unto Him who is able to do exceedingly abundantly above all that we ask or think, according to the power that works in us,

21 to Him be glory in the church by Christ Jesus to all generations, forever and ever. Amen

Hallelujah! God will establish the prayer of the righteous!

The prayer of Thanksgiving

The Jewish culture and Gods´ commandments reinforced the offering of thanksgiving as a way of life. The Gentiles did not have that custom, so the Apostle Paul introduced it to the gentile churches in powerful practical revelation. He wrote to the Philippians:

Philippians 4:6-7
6 Be anxious for nothing, but in everything by prayer and supplication, with thanksgiving, let your requests be made known to God;
7 and the peace of God, which surpasses all understanding, will guard your hearts and minds through Christ Jesus.

Prayer and supplication, blended with thanksgiving, enable us to escape the pressure of anxiety and fear, and live in the Peace of God.

There is peace with God that is given us through the sacrifice of Jesus. God is not opposing us anymore. That is true whether we are aware of it or not. But the Peace of God is God's own peace imparted into our hearts and minds.

Jesus promised to give us His Peace. He said that it would not come to us as the world gives and receives peace. His peace comes as His own gift to those that draw near to Him in prayer. Jesus said:

John 14:27
"Peace I leave with you, My peace I give to you; not as the world gives do I give to you. Let not your heart be troubled, neither let it be afraid.

Troubled and anxious hearts have difficulty asking with confidence and faith. And those who pray the "asking prayer" of supplication must ask in faith in order to receive.

Our answers are not usually as simple as we might think. For that reason the answers to many of our prayers come as a complicated dealing of God on many levels.

The prayer for wisdom is a good example, because wisdom is not simple.

The Apostle James explained the need for faith when dealing with the issue of godly wisdom. In order for God to give wisdom to a foolish person, He must move in many areas of their lives. He has to purify motives, correct errors in understanding, and establish the foundations necessary for wisdom to be pure and without selfishness. Wisdom is a very big issue. It will take time and process. So James wrote:

James 1:5-8
5 If any of you lacks wisdom, let him ask of God, who gives to all liberally and without reproach, and it will be given to him.
6 But let him ask in faith, with no doubting, for he who doubts is like a wave of the sea driven and tossed by the wind.
7 For let not that man suppose that he will receive anything from the Lord;
8 he is a double-minded man, unstable in all his ways.

The peace of God lays the very foundation for being led of the Spirit into and through the refining and renewing processes necessary for wisdom to be imparted.

It takes a strong measure of the peace of God to walk through this level of process.

The same is true with many other kinds of requests.

When we ask for a loved one to be saved, God must move through life's circumstances and deal with many secret issues. He must honor that person's own right of decision. Many times He must work through other people. It will take time and organized strategy to bring that person to a time of spiritual decision.

The person praying for them must maintain confidence and faith, being willing to continue in supplication while the process continues. Sometimes, if the person is close to the person praying, they may even suffer because of the pressure God brings to bear on the one being prayed for.

Notice the three blended parts of the kind of prayer given us in Philippians: Prayer, which is the prayer of relationship and communion; supplication, which is the prayer of "asking in correct attitude and order;" and "thanksgiving" that invites God's peace and enables us to live in that peace while God moves in and around us.

Thanksgiving prayer helps us escape anxiety by bringing to remembrance the faithfulness of God in past times of emergency and need. It helps us see things through a better perspective.

Asking in Jesus' Name

Asking God for the things we need is invited by the Lord. Remember, Jesus told us to ask:

Luke 11:9
"So I say to you, ask, and it will be given to you; seek, and you will find; knock, and it will be opened to you.

Then, with the Disciples at the last supper He instructed them to ask in His Name:

John 14:13-14
13 "And whatever you ask in My name, that I will do, that the Father may be glorified in the Son.

14 "If you ask anything in My name, I will do it.

John 16:23-24
23 "And in that day you will ask Me nothing. Most assuredly, I say to you, whatever you ask the Father in My name He will give you.
24 "Until now you have asked nothing in My name. Ask, and you will receive, that your joy may be full.

Asking prayer must be offered in the correct motivation.

Asking "in the name of" another person means to ask under their authority.

Using someone else's name for authority purposes has strict guidelines of purpose. If you have authority within your employment to spend money, or use other people to accomplish things, you must be sure that you exercise that authority within the regulations and purposes of the company you work for.

Your authority is confined to the issues authorized. It is the same in the Kingdom of God. To place Jesus' Holy Name upon our own selfish purposes is to misuse our authority and to take His Name in vain.

James speaks to this issue calling it asking "amiss".

James 4:1-3
1 Where do wars and fights come from among you? Do they not come from your desires for pleasure that war in your members?
2 You lust and do not have. You murder and covet and cannot obtain. You fight and war. Yet you do not have because you do not ask.
3 You ask and do not receive, because you ask amiss, that you may spend it on your pleasures.

Asking *"amiss"* is the result of leading selfish lives. It reveals that we have not fully surrendered to God. For this very reason we are to begin our prayer agenda with the issues of laying down our own personal desires, and seeking to establish His kingdom.

Questions to ponder:

1. Do you pray with praise and thanksgiving?

2. Do you pray asking for forgiveness according to your own acts of forgiveness?

3. Do you sense an "entering into the Spirit" when you pray?

4. Can you see that praying selfishly reveals the need for repentance from selfish living and selfish motives?

Chapter 6
All kinds of Prayer - III

The "casting" prayer

There are two Greek words that are translated prayer in our English Bibles. They are the words "proseuche" and "deesis". "Proseuche" is used more often than "deesis" by far. The meaning of "proseuche" is "to pour out" while the "deesis" prayer is the prayer of petition.

Many have not learned how to pray the "pouring out" prayer. Instead, they try to pray with all kinds of suppressed feelings and emotions inside them.

We must learn that our prayer of communion and fellowship with God must be a sharing of what is deep within us. It is this level of sharing that enables us to enter into deep intimacy with God.

Within the scope of the "pouring out prayers", we find the "casting prayer". This is the prayer that is used to "cast" our problems on the Lord in such a way that we are released from them emotionally and become free of worry and concern.

We find this kind of prayer mentioned in the first Epistle of Peter. It is part of Peter's answer to the difficult problems the Church was encountering, as Gentile opposition began to increase dramatically.

The believers around Rome were experiencing heavy opposition from without, while God was purging and cleansing from within. It was a difficult and confusing time.

They were dealing with corruption and evil from their political leaders, while God was asking for a submission to those in authority. Their gatherings were being outlawed. Their belongings were being confiscated. Loved ones were being persecuted and scattered, even killed. When they were accepted they had to work as slaves.

Peter's advice to them was to maintain submission in all relationships.

1 Peter 2:13-14
13 Therefore submit yourselves to every ordinance of man for the Lord's sake, whether to the king as supreme,
14 or to governers, as to those who are sent by him...

Verse 18 Servants, be submissive to your masters with all fear, not only to the good and gentle, but also to the harsh.

1 Peter 5:5
Likewise you younger people, submit yourselves to your elders. Yes, all of you be submissive to one another, and be clothed with humility, for

> *"God resists the proud,*
> *But gives grace to the humble."*

Submission to sinful authority figures can be very hard and many times even injurious. Dealing with the frustrations of continuing to do what is right when others are taking advantage of you is fierce spiritual warfare.

Peter tells them what to do:

1 Peter 5:6-11
6 Therefore humble yourselves under the mighty hand of God, that He may exalt you in due time,
7 casting all your care upon Him, for He cares for you.
8 Be sober, be vigilant; because your adversary the devil walks about like a roaring lion, seeking whom he may devour.
9 Resist him, steadfast in the faith, knowing that the same sufferings are experienced by your brotherhood in the world.
10 But may the God of all grace, who called us to His eternal glory by Christ Jesus, after you have suffered a while, perfect, establish,

strengthen, and settle you.
11 to Him be the glory and the dominion forever and ever. Amen.

In their situation these words were much more than beautiful and poetic words from their minister. They were life-giving instructions on how to survive the most intense of struggles.

They needed to see that behind the scenes Satan was the one they were dealing with. Even though people were his tools, the real enemy was Satan. They needed to keep in mind that he would win if they would react to their situation sinfully.

They had to realize that God was also present and that He would accomplish His purposes in the very midst of these conflicts. They must stay on course no matter what happened.

The answer was given in this simple message. It was founded upon two powerful principles; the power of humility and the effect of the "casting prayer."

* *Humble yourselves under the mighty hand of God -*

* *casting all your care upon Him, He cares for you.*

Humbling ourselves means to submit to circumstances that we have no power over, as unto God Himself. It means to go through them without rebellion or sinning.

Because of the powerful emotions and anxieties these kinds of circumstances can provoke in us, we must have an outlet. That outlet is "casting our care upon Him".

The reason we can do this in confidence is *"for He cares for you."*

We must believe that, for He does care for us. He not only cares for us, He cares about everything that goes on about us.

That is why we can submit to Him in everything and cast our care upon Him.

This "care casting" is done in prayer. It is the act of bringing those things that are troubling us to Him in a "pouring out" of our emotions and feelings.

The Spirit of God takes these issues and gives us His peace and confidence in their place. It is a great exchange.

David, the great King of Israel, was a man who wrote and sang his prayers to God. They were preserved for us in the book of Psalms. In them we can see many occasions of this kind of prayer.

He was persecuted, his enemies were very real. They sought to kill him out of jealousy. He responded in submission to God, but he also "cast his care" upon the Lord.

Listen to him pray:

When he fled from Absalom, his own son, who had taken the kingdom from him:

Psalm 3:1-4
1 Lord, how they have increased who trouble me!
Many are they who rise up against me.
2 Many are they who say of me,
"There is no help for him in God." Selah

3 But you, O Lord, are a shield for me,
My glory and the One who lifts up my head
4 I cried to the Lord with my voice,
And He heard me from His holy hill.

We can see in this prayer the pouring out of his personal pain, and the almost immediate response of the Spirit in making him aware of God's provision of help.

Psalm 13

1 How long, O Lord?
Will you forget me forever?
How long will you hide Your face from me?
2 How long shall I take counsel in my soul,
Having sorrow in my heart daily?
How long will my enemy be exalted over me?

3 Consider and hear me, O Lord my God;
Enlighten my eyes,
Lest I sleep the sleep of death;
4 Lest my enemy say,
"I have prevailed against him."
Lest those who trouble me rejoice when I am moved.

5 But I have trusted in Your mercy;
My heart shall rejoice in Your salvation.
6 I will sing to the Lord,
Because He has dealt bountifully with me.

We can see that as he poured out his true feelings, God responded by giving him renewed confidence in his heart.

Psalm 25:16-21

16 Turn Yourself to me, and have mercy on me,
For I am desolate and afflicted.
17 The troubles of my heart have enlarged;
Bring me out of my distress!
18 Look on my affliction and my pain,
And forgive all my sins.
19 Consider my enemies, for they are many;
And they hate me with cruel hatred.
20 Keep my soul, and deliver me;
Let me not be ashamed, for I put my trust in You.
21 Let integrity and uprightness preserve me,
For I wait for You.

There are many more Psalms that reveal the power of this kind of praying. But these reveal the principle of sharing deep emotional distress before God in a way that removes it from our own shoulders and replaces it with God's peace and confidence.

The "casting prayer" is explicit enough about the problem so that it enables the person praying to completely leave it with the Lord.

The result is that they are left with clear remembrance of the faithfulness and awesome power of the Lord. In that frame of reference, their own problems become small and they can begin to praise Him, and trust Him in confidence.

Prayer for Enemies

Even though some of the "cares" we spoke about earlier concern what others do to us. It is important to understand how to pray for enemies.

At the very beginning of their training, Jesus taught his Disciples the importance of this kind of prayer. It was a change from what was understood in their day.

The common attitude towards enemies was to "hate" them. The refrain was "you shall love your neighbor and hate your enemies." Some religions of our own time continue in this concept thinking it to be Godly.

Jesus corrected that error, and then taught His disciples what attitudes and actions we must take to free ourselves from the defiling effects of other's conduct toward us.

Matthew 5:43-48
43" You have heard that it was said, 'you shall love your neighbor and hate your enemy.'
44 "But I say to you, love your enemies, bless those who curse you, do good to those who hate you, and pray for those who spitefully use you and persecute you,

45 that you may be sons of your Father in heaven; For He makes His sun rise on the evil and on the good, and sends rain on the just and on the unjust.
46 "For if you love those who love you, what reward have you? Do not even the tax collectors do the same?
47 "And if you greet your brethren only, what do you do more than others? Do not even the tax collectors do so?
48 "Therefore you shall be perfect, just as your Father in heaven is perfect."

Notice this same context in *Luke 6:27-36*. Only here Jesus is quoted as saying: *"Therefore be merciful, just as your Father is also merciful"*, rather than *"be perfect."*

Defining Who Are Our Enemies

It is important to clearly understand what the Scripture intends. In this case the subject is the disciple's response toward their enemies. However, if you are not clear on who your enemies are, you will not be able to take appropriate action.

Jesus shows who He defines as enemies by dealing with three issues.

* Enemies are those who *"curse you"*,

* those who *"hate you"*,

* and those who *"spitefully use you."*

Cursing in this context does not mean to put a hex on you through witchcraft. It does not mean to speak to you with cursing or bad language. It means to speak against you.

To hate in this context is not speaking of hatred of emotions but of desiring evil to happen to you. Hatred produces evil intentions and rejection.

To spitefully use you means to misuse you spitefully. It involves twisting words, taking advantage of human weaknesses in order to impugn with the stain of unrighteousness. It speaks of misusing relationship in a damaging and spiteful way.

If Satan can not encourage us to sin from our own desires and lusts, he will try to cause us to sin in reaction to others. Actions of cursing, hatefulness, and spite, are strategies to provoke a reaction of the flesh. Therefore Jesus teaches us what the correct reaction should be.

It is not enough to be able to refrain from evil responses. We must learn to respond correctly.

First we need to "Love our enemies."

To love them we have to identify them. It is clear from Scripture that Jesus means our enemies are those who do one or more of these things. Those who curse you, hate you, and spitefully use you.

Then He shows us that each one of these negative actions requires a positive action from us in return.

If we remain inactive, we run the risk of allowing our hurts to turn into bitterness and resentment. We will suffer from the confusion of trying to understand why they treat us so badly. This in turn moves us away from the Holy Spirit. Instead, we must move away from the offense and hurt or it will cling to us. We can move away from it by refusing to respond in like kind. Then we can forgive them and purpose to love them.

To love means to commit to the highest good. It means to seek only what is best for the person. Therefore we do not lend our tongues to speak evil, only blessing. This is the action that defeats cursing.

Hatred is overcome by positive actions. We are to do good to them in return. That means we seek opportunity to do something that will benefit them. This positive action defeats the spiritual force behind hatred.

We are to pray for those who spitefully use us. Praying for them may not always involve praying for blessing. It may involve praying for repentance or chastisement. This would be the highest good for them. For, if they do not repent they will endure severe chastisement from God.

Be careful, this process can easily be a justification for unforgiveness. The best prayer is made after forgiveness and our love commitment is reestablished.

Praying for God to intervene in human abuse is the best way to defeat its purpose, because it turns action over to the Lord. It gives vent to dangerous hurt. And it allows us to be healed in the presence of the Lord.

The "pouring out" of painful emotions in prayer keeps us from being overcome by evil, and invites God's Spirit to bring us holy comfort.

The Apostle Paul wrote:

Romans 12:17-21
17 Repay no one evil for evil. Have regard for good things in the sight of all men.
18 If it is possible, as much as depends on you, live peaceably with all men.
19 Beloved, do not avenge yourselves, but rather give place to wrath; for it is written, "Vengeance is Mine, I will repay," says the Lord.
20 Therefore:

> *"If your enemy is hungry, feed him;*
> *If he is thirsty, give him a drink;*
> *For in so doing you will heap coals of fire on his head."*

21 Do not be overcome by evil, but overcome evil with good.

To *"give place to wrath"*, is to turn the wrath issue over to God through prayer. It is not good for us to carry anger in any form. God alone can minister wrath and mercy in fairness and grace.

By releasing our anger in prayer, we are delivered from wrath and anger, and enabled to do good things instead of evil. In this way God is moved to act on our behalf.

The Prophet Isaiah wrote hundreds of years earlier:

Isaiah 54:16-17
16 "Behold, I have created the blacksmith
Who blows the coals in the fire,
Who brings forth an instrument for his work;
And I have created the spoiler to destroy.
17 No weapon formed against you shall prosper,
And every tongue which rises against you in judgment
You shall condemn.
This is the heritage of the servants of the LORD,
And their righteousness is from Me," Says the LORD.

Our response to condemning tongues and their poison is to take it before the Lord. We spiritually condemn the unrighteous tongue by refusing to respond in like kind. By so doing the issue is left in God's Presence. And He said that He will correct His own.

The recorded prayers of David are clear examples of this kind of prayer:

Psalm 5:8-12
8 Lead me, O Lord, in Your righteousness because of my enemies;
Make Your way straight before my face.
9 For there is no faithfulness in their mouth;
Their inward part is destruction;
Their throat is an open tomb;
They flatter with their tongue.
10 Pronounce them guilty, O God!
Let them fall by their own counsels;
Cast them out in the multitude of their transgressions.

For they have rebelled against You.
11 *But let all those rejoice who put their trust in You;*
Let them ever shout for joy, because You defend them;
Let those also who love Your name
Be joyful in You.
12 *For you, O Lord, will bless the righteous;*
With favor You will surround him as with a shield.

In this Psalm we can hear David asking for punishment on those who oppose him and blessing on those who serve the Lord. By casting his feelings and personal opinions about the situation on the Lord, he was freed to rejoice in God's faithfulness and blessing. He was also able to accept God's actions as right and righteous in the situation.

Praying for enemies is powerful prayer.

Questions to ponder:

1. Have you ever experienced the release from casting your care upon the Lord?

2. Have you ever taken your enemies before the Lord in prayer?

3. If so, did you experience release from the evil which was intended by them?

4. Have you ever experienced restoration in difficult relationships because you took them to the Lord?

Chapter 7
Prayers of the Holy Spirit

Groanings of the Spirit

When Paul in *Romans 7 and 8* wrote about the conflict between the flesh and Spirit, he also explained one of the ways the Holy Spirit helps us through praying.

Romans 8:26-27
26 Likewise the Spirit also helps in our weaknesses. For we do not know what we should pray for as we ought, but the Spirit Himself makes intercession for us with groanings which cannot be uttered.
27 Now he who searches the hearts knows what the mind of the Spirit is, because He makes intercession for the saints according to the will of God.

The NIV translation expresses it this way:

"He intercedes for us with groans that words cannot express."

The prayer of groaning was seen in Jesus earthly ministry when he raised Lazarus from the dead. Mary and Martha met him before He came to the tomb where they had laid his body. They both dumped their own sorrow, grief and hurt on Him while He endeavored to comfort them and maintain His focus on what the Father was instructing Him to do. The Holy Spirit had rested upon Him, and He groaned in the Spirit on two occasions. It was a groaning of discontent with the situation at hand. There was even a note of irritation in the meaning of the word.

John 11:33, 38
33 Therefore when Jesus saw her weeping, and the Jews who came with her weeping, He groaned in the spirit and was troubled.

38 Then Jesus, again groaning in Himself, came to the tomb....

Many times the Holy Spirit prays through us with the same kinds of groaning. They are groans of unrest with things as they are. It is a kind of prayer that cannot be verbalized, yet in it there is deep longing for God to move in our situations. It comes from deep within our hearts and specifically from the heart of the Holy Spirit.

Jesus' earthly prayer life was full of this kind of earnest emotion. The writer of Hebrews tells us:

Hebrews 5:7
In the days of His flesh, when He had offered up prayers and supplications, with vehement cries and tears to Him who was able to save Him from death, and was heard because of His godly fear.

There is evidence that Moses also groaned in the Spirit when he was interceding for Israel after they had formed and then worshipped the golden calf.

Exodus 32:32
"Yet now, if You will forgive their sin—but if not, I pray, blot me out of Your book which You have written."

The marks "—" in the text explain that Moses used words or language that could not be translated. It was the very first occasion of spiritual intercession. Moses was offering his own life for the salvation of his people.

Groaning in the Spirit often accompanies the prayer of intercession.

There is groaning also in our own spirits, calling out for the change that God has promised us. It comes from the deep desire for what is to be our destiny. It seeks to propel us toward God with greater intensity than our minds or our natural emotions can muster or express. The Apostle Paul explained:

Romans 8:23
Not only that, but we also who have the firstfruits of the Spirit, even we ourselves groan within ourselves, eagerly waiting for the adoption, the redemption of our body.

This groaning prayer is the natural response of our own spirits to the decadence and corruption we sense all around us. Inside us the renewing process is going on. Yet it seems so slow. The desire to be fully changed produces a kind of spiritual discontent. Our spirits desire to change without delay, while our minds and our experience move so slowly.

Spiritual groaning is a very holy thing. Do not be afraid of it. However, it is a very private kind of prayer. Remember, Jesus separated Himself from the Disciples while He prayed in agony in the Garden.

Prayer with unknown Tongues

In *1 Corinthians 14* we learn very practical things about prayer in tongues. It is also called prayer in the Spirit (the Holy Spirit) and prayer with the spirit (my own spirit). It is a prayer that my own spirit makes through the enablement of the Holy Spirit in an unknown language.

Even though the purpose of *Chapter 14* is to correct misuse of spiritual gifts, as Paul speaks of tongues, he gives us clear understanding of the benefits and characteristics of tongues as an aid to our prayer life. Therefore, omitting the corrections we glean some very clear insights.

1 Corinthians 14:2, 4, 5, 14, 15, 18, 37, 39
2 For he who speaks in a tongue does not speak to men but to God, for no one understands him; however, in the spirit he speaks mysteries.

4 He who speaks in a tongue edifies himself, ...

5 I wish you all spoke with tongues, ...

14 For if I pray in a tongue, my spirit prays, but my understanding is unfruitful.

15 What is the conclusion then? I will pray with the spirit, and I will also pray with the understanding. I will sing with the spirit, and I will also sing with the understanding.

18 I thank my God I speak with tongues more than you all.

37 If anyone thinks himself to be a prophet or spiritual, let him acknowledge that the things which I write to you are the commandments of the Lord.

39 Therefore, brethren, desire earnestly to prophesy, and do not forbid to speak with tongues.

Praying in tongues is a spiritual tool God gives to help us enter deeply into the realm of the Spirit. All of the spiritual gifts, graces, and manifestations are spiritual helps and tools to aid us to go beyond the limitation of our human minds and their limited thinking ability, and into deep and precious communion with the Holy Spirit.

We need not fear them as long as our hearts are earnestly seeking God and His will.

Spiritual gifts are given for our benefit. They are precious.

Error in spiritual gifts comes from having selfish or prideful motivations.

1 Corinthians 14 clearly teaches that spiritual utterances must be held up to judgment for this very reason. It also maintains that the focus of those ministering, as well as the utterances themselves, must be on edification and comfort. When this is the basic agenda, we need not fear spiritual gifts.

3 But he who prophesies speaks edification and exhortation and comfort to men.

12 Even so you, since you are zealous for spiritual gifts, let it be for the edification of the church that you seek to excel.

26 ...Let all things be done for edification.

Prayer in tongues is a rich privilege. The Apostle Paul, who we know as a no nonsense man of wisdom and focus, said that he prayed in tongues more than any one in Corinth. It was obviously one of the secrets of his spiritual strength and endurance.

Today speaking in tongues is a much maligned and denigrated way of praying. Tongues are even called the least of the gifts. There is no Scripture context for this action or statement. God only gives good and perfect gifts. They are all important, or He would not give them. The misuse of some, or the bad attitude of some, should not hinder the rest from the truth.

God wants all of us to speak in tongues. This fact is very evident when we consider that all of the 120 gathered in the upper room on the Day of Pentecost spoke in tongues, all those gathered in Cornelius' house spoke in tongues, and all who were present in the first outpouring of the Holy Spirit in Ephesus spoke in tongues. All of those outpourings were significant in setting the foundation for New Testament practice. In this way the Holy Scriptures reveal that all believers have the privilege of prayer with their spirit in angelic or heavenly tongues because of God's goodness, grace and mercy.

When we read the express desire of Paul in Verse 5 and the explanation of authority in context, you can see that his desire was in reality the expression of the Lord's desire.

1 Corinthians 14:5, 37
5 I wish you all spoke with tongues...

37 If anyone thinks himself to be a prophet or spiritual, let him acknowledge that the things which I write to you are the commandments of the Lord.

Spiritual Prayer

Jude 20
But you, beloved, building yourselves up on your most holy faith, praying in the Holy Spirit,

Prayers of the Holy Spirit, or prayer and singing in the spirit, build powerful relationships with God. They are meant to build up the believer, and tear down spiritual strongholds.

Do not put them in a place of lesser value than prayers of understanding. As we learn to fully walk in the Spirit, they will take a more powerful place to prepare us and equip us for service.

Questions to ponder:

1. Have you been afraid of prayers of the Holy Spirit? If so, why?

2. Have you mistaken the groaning of your spirit to be depression or sorrow?

3. Have you mistakenly called praying in tongues "foolishness", or even "devlish"?

4. Could the fear and confusion over spiritual gifts, and especially praying in tongues be partly to blame for the carnality and personal failures among Christians today? How?

Chapter 8
The Word of God in the Holy Scriptures

The Bible is the inspired record of God's continual revelation of Himself, His Nature, Character, and Will.

The book we call the Bible is in fact a "library" of sacred writings. Each book was written in a different time and place. They were written by different men who, in their own circumstances, were moved upon by the Holy Spirit. These sacred writings were preserved and passed down to the next generations. In time these scrolls and books were growing in number and there was a need to verify which of them were in fact divinely inspired.

They were held up to intense historic scrutiny and prophetic judgment. Those writings that passed these tests were put together and kept as divinely inspired and honored as God's Word to men.

Today, we accept 66 books of the Old and New Testament as the divinely inspired Word of God. We call it the Bible.

Our own life experiences are proof enough of its inspiration and veracity.

But how is it applied to our lives today?

What is the best process for understanding it?

What place should God's Word have in our lives?

The Bible speaks about itself.

The Apostle Paul, speaking of the Old Testament Scriptures, reminded

Timothy of the wealth that was his because of the Holy Scriptures he had learned as a child. Then he explained its usefulness.

2 Timothy 3:14-17
14 But you must continue in the things which you have learned and been assured of, knowing from whom you have learned them,
15 and that from childhood you have known the Holy Scriptures, which are able to make you wise for salvation through faith which is in Christ Jesus.
16 All Scripture is given by inspiration of God, and is profitable for doctrine, for reproof, for correction, for instruction in righteousness.
17 that the man of God may be complete, thoroughly equipped for every good work.

The Apostle Peter was witness to God's audible voice. It happened during the time of Jesus' transfiguration. Peter was one of the three Disciples Jesus had invited to go with Him. It was there on the mount of transfiguration that The Father spoke to them from heaven regarding His Son Jesus. The story is found in:

Mark 9:2-4
2 Now after six days Jesus took Peter, James, and John, and led them up on a high mountain apart by themselves; and He was transfigured before them.
3 His clothes became shining, exceedingly white, like snow, such as no launderer on earth can whiten them.
4 And Elijah appeared to them with Moses, and they were talking with Jesus.

Peter was so moved that after they finished talking he spoke up:

Verses 5-7
5 Then Peter answered and said to Jesus, "Rabbi, it is good for us to be here; and let us make three tabernacles: one for You, one for Moses, and one for Elijah" —
6 because he did not know what to say, for they were greatly afraid.
7 And a cloud came and overshadowed them; and a voice came out of

the cloud, saying, "This is My beloved Son. Hear Him!"

Peter had witnessed other occasions when The Father had spoken audibly to Jesus, one of those being the time He spoke from heaven at Jesus baptism. He mentioned these two occasions later on:

2 Peter 1:16-21
16 For we did not follow cunningly devised fables when we made known to you the power and coming of our Lord Jesus Christ, but were eyewitnesses of His majesty.
17 For He received from God the Father honor and glory when such a voice came to Him from the Excellent Glory: "This is My beloved Son, in whom I am well pleased."
18 And we heard this voice which came from heaven when we were with Him on the holy mountain.
19 And so we have the prophetic word confirmed, which you do well to heed as a light that shines in a dark place, until the day dawns and the morning star rises in your hearts;
20 knowing this first, that no prophecy of Scripture is of any private interpretation,
21 for prophecy never came by the will of man, but holy men of God spoke as they were moved by the Holy Spirit.

Peter calls the Gospel, *"the prophetic word confirmed"*. It is so powerful and accurate that *"you do well to heed as a light that shines in a dark place, until the day dawns and the morning star rises in your hearts"*.

He had actually heard God speak audibly, but he placed the Word of God that was given prophetically on an even higher plane.

Human weakness, imagination, filtering, and weak memory, all can bring distortion to audible communication from God. This is exactly why God wrote the Ten Commandments with his own hand and gave them to Moses. Then Moses was commanded to write all that God said, and preserve it for the people of Israel.

In time the prophets were given visitations of the Holy Spirit, helped, directed, and even visited by angels. They were commanded and inspired to write their messages in many ways.

The Epistle of Hebrews begins with these words:

Hebrews 1:1
God, who at various times and in different ways spoke in time past to the fathers by the prophets...

The fact is that God spoke to the Fathers.

The Scriptures are the written Word of God!

1 Peter 1: 21
...for prophecy never came by the will of man, but holy men of God spoke as they were moved by the Holy Spirit.

Because the Holy Spirit is the inspiration and motivator of the Scriptures, we can be sure that He will always move in agreement with the Scriptures.

The Scriptures contain the Word of God in human situations.

"Logos" and "Rhema"

There are two important Greek words translated as "word" in our English Bibles. They give us a more clear understanding of the way God's Word works in us. They are "Logos" and "Rhema".

Logos - message - speaks more of the over-all message of God. It is generally used to speak of the over-all revelation of the Scriptures.

The writer of the Book of Hebrews uses this word to reveal the power of the Word in this form.

Hebrews 4:12
For the word of God is living and powerful, and sharper than any two-edged sword, piercing even to the division of soul and spirit, and of joints and marrow, and is a discerner of the thoughts and intents of the heart.

In Matthew 13, Jesus called the Word of God (the Logos), the seed of the Kingdom.

It was the word used to describe the Apostles preaching:

Acts 4:31
... and they were all filled with the Holy Spirit, and they spoke the word of God with boldness.

The "rhema" (a matter, or topic) - differs from "logos" in that it seems to be the "freshly spoken", personalized word, that comes through a message of Scripture, a prophecy, or even by means of a thought in our hearts.

This is a personal "Word of God" to you for your particular problem or need right now!

It is the "rhema" that brings faith to our hearts! We see it used powerfully in:

Romans 10:17
So then faith comes by hearing, and hearing by the word of God.

This Scripture reveals the interplay between the "logos" and the "rhema".

By exposing ourselves to the "logos" or message, the Spirit of God will specially "breath upon" or inspire us regarding specific issues, and produce faith through this process.

In a way it can be said that the Spirit of God, moving upon the "logos" will speak a "rhema" into our hearts. Faith springs from this process.

Jesus Himself is the "Logos of God!"

John 1:1, 14
1 In the beginning was the Word, and the Word was with God, and the Word was God.

14 And the Word became flesh and dwelt among us, and we beheld his glory, the glory as of the only begotten of the Father, full of grace and truth.

In this respect Jesus is the "Living Word of God." That is, He is the fullest expression of all that God is. And, He is the means of God's expression to men.

The writer of Hebrews comments:

Hebrews 1:1-3
1 God, who at various times and in various ways spoke in time past to the fathers by the prophets,
2 has in these last days spoken to us by His Son, whom He has appointed heir of all things, through whom also He made the worlds.
3 who being the brightness of His glory and the express image of His person, and upholding all things by the word of His power, when He had by Himself purged our sins, sat down at the right hand of the Majesty on high.

The Word has a powerful effect on our lives. The Word is the Holy Seed and cause of our faith. Jesus' own person is contained in the deposit of the Word in the new creature within us. It is His Spirit and divine nature that it brings. Peter wrote:

2 Peter 1:4
...by which have been given to us exceedingly great and precious promises, that through these you may be partakers of the divine nature,...

The Apostle Paul wrote:

2 Corinthians 3:18
But we all, with unveiled face, beholding as in a mirror the glory of the Lord, are being transformed into the same image from glory to glory, just as by the Spirit of the Lord.

The safety of Scripture

The Holy Scriptures are given to us for the purpose of keeping us within the confines of historical doctrines and Testimony. Every doctrinal fallacy and tendency to go astray, every work of the flesh, and every kind of rebellion, is exposed by the Holy Scriptures. Therefore an understanding of the Bible is necessary in the life of the Christian.

King David wrote:

Psalm 119:11
Your word I have hidden in my heart,
That I might not sin against You.

The preaching of the Word

Preaching is a powerful expression of the Word of God. When believers meet together and bring the "Logos" and the "Rhema" of the Living Word to each other in the atmosphere of worship and surrender, powerful life changes take place. People joined together to worship God and to hear the Word are what our meetings are all about.

These meetings provide a more powerful expression of His presence than when we are alone. It is what makes the Church gathering so important. God's respect for meetings of this kind is why so much happens to those who attend them. It is also why attending Church regularly is encouraged by Scripture.

The writer of Hebrews admonished:

Hebrews 10:25

...not forsaking the assembling of ourselves together, as is the manner of some, but exhorting one another, and so much the more as you see the Day approaching.

Much is accomplished in the lives of those who gather together and submit themselves to the exposure of the preaching, teaching, and exhortation of the Word of God.

The carnal mind does not understand this.

1 Corinthians 1:18
For the message (preaching KJV) of the cross is foolishness to those who are perishing, but to us who are being saved it is the power of God.

Most of us can testify that many of the greatest experiences of our lives happened as we experienced God's presence in a preaching service.

Most of us made the final decision to trust in Jesus as the result of hearing God's Word preached. Many other important issues are addressed by the Spirit of God when we are together and expectant under the preaching of the Word of God

We have heard the Spirit's voice calling us to greater consecrations.

We have been healed as we heard the Word and responded.

We have received wisdom and direction.

We have been comforted.

We have avoided terrible mistakes by God's intervention.

All these kinds of things happen when we gather together and humble ourselves before the Word of God.

Exposing ourselves to the Word of God by reading in our own devotions and participating in preaching and teaching services are the seeding times for the changing power of God in our lives.

Reading, meditating in, and hearing the Word of God expounded, bring the history of God's dealing with man, the message of deliverance, the warnings to men and women of other times, and the testimonies of their salvation or failures, into a focused impartation of life and wisdom for us today.

The Christian that takes these lightly has limited himself to mediocrity and stunted his or her growth in the realm of the spirit.

He has taken himself out of God's nourishment program. He will become a spiritual weakling.

Satan's strategy

It is for this reason that Satan encourages us to shorten the times of the Word. The carnal mind wants to limit us to a favorite verse of Scripture each day rather than a true immersion in the Word. The strategy of the carnal mind seeks to limit the preaching services to 15 or 20 minutes.

We could not learn mathematics if we did not study every day and for years.

It would involve home work.

We would have to pay attention to lectures.

The same goes for spelling, or reading, or anything else of value we want to learn.

Why is it that the Word of God is given such a low place?

If we wanted to learn any other skill or issue of consequence we would not limit the learning time to 20 or 30 minutes. And we would not shrink back from the learning experience if the teacher was not funny, or charismatic, or did not tell emotional stories to entertain us.

The reason behind this carnal mind set about the preaching and teaching of God's Word is a strategy of Satan to weaken the effect of the Word by diminishing its sense of importance in real and practical ways.

Seed and Soil Condition

When Jesus called the Word "seed", He opened our understanding to know that all the rules of seed apply. The amount you sow determines the amount you will receive in harvest. If our harvest of spiritual change is small, it is probably because we have not planted much spiritual seed.

But there is another issue that Jesus covered by teaching in parable form. It is the condition of our own hearts. Jesus revealed that our own hearts need preparation for the Word to have its most powerful results.

Matthew 13:3-9
3 Then He spoke many things to them in parables, saying "Behold a sower went out to sow.
4 "And as he sowed, some seed fell by the wayside; and the birds came and devoured them.
5 "Some fell on stony places, where they did not have much earth; and they immediately sprang up because they had no depth of earth.
6 "But when the sun was up they were scorched, and because they had no root they withered away.
7 "And some fell among thorns, and the thorns sprang up and choked them.
8 "But others fell on good ground and yielded a crop: some a hundredfold, some sixty, some thirty..
9 "He who has ears to hear, let him hear!"

The meaning of this parable is given to us in *Verses 18-23*.

Jesus used the four kinds of soil condition to explain why the Word produces differently in each person.

There are four basic responses to the Word. These are all determined by preconditions upon which the seed of the Word falls.

1. **Hard ground** The *"wayside"* was the fringes of the fields that were used for pathways and left unplowed. It is ground that is not prepared for seed and is hardened by much traffic.

The *"birds of the air"* are seen as the demonic forces that snatch the seed from this soil before it has a chance to penetrate and bring life.

Seed will not just lay there. If you do not receive it at once, if you decide to wait and procrastinate, spiritual law gives that seed up to Satan's hosts, to take it away from the memory and decision process.

2. **Stony places** - (*stony ground*) is the person that has issues that won't yield to the seed. They are usually areas of bitterness, unforgiveness, rebellion, grudges, anger, and the like.

The soil around them may be good but when the seed seeks to send out roots, these unrepentant areas limit the rooting process and the slightest problem causes bitterness to spill over and stunt its growth.

These believers are barely alive, and never fruitful.

It is not because the Seed is not strong. It is because they have not given the seed the right kind of place in their lives.

3. **Thorny ground** - (*among thorns*) is the person that receives the seed but refuses to give it first place. He still gives equal place to *"the worries of life and deceitfulness of wealth."* These grow together and the bad seed chokes the good seed so that it becomes too weak to produce fruit.

These people are also alive spiritually but are never able to be fruitful. Again, the problem is not with the seed but the place of importance that each person gives the Word.

4. **Good ground** This has the potential to produce in three dimensions of fruitfulness. 100 fold, 60 fold, and 30 fold harvests.

Jesus told us what kind of people will harvest 100 fold:

Matthew 19:29
"And everyone who has left houses or brothers or sisters or father or

mother or wife or children or lands, for My name's sake, shall receive a hundredfold, and inherit eternal life.

So the 100 fold effect of the Word comes to those who have denied themselves and followed Jesus. This kind of heart is like the good ground that can produce powerfully.

The 60 fold harvest is for those who serve the Lord, but not sacrificially. And the 30 fold harvest is left for those who live mostly for themselves and their own family.

Jesus was showing that The Word of God has powerful potential to make life worth living. But the conditions of each person's heart, and the willingness each one brings to the seed of the Word, will affect its power in our lives.

Which kind of soil does your heart represent?

Our hearts "soil condition" is something that can only be changed on an individual basis. Only you can deal with what is in your heart. I am the only one that can deal with mine.

Jesus will not change what we do not release to Him.

Questions to ponder:

1. Are you convinced that the Bible contains the Word of God?

2. What place do you give it in your allocation of time and energy?

3. Do you think you need to place yourself and your family under Spirit led and empowered teachers and leaders?

4. What is the condition of the "soil" of your heart?

5. Is your heart prepared for a strong harvest of change and blessing?

Chapter 9
Faith

Faith provides the access to all of God's grace and provision. Therefore, it is impossible
to walk in the Spirit without walking in faith, for faith is the basis of all relationship with God.

The Apostle Paul wrote the Ephesian believers:

Ephesians 2:8-9
8 For by grace you have been saved through faith, and that not of yourselves; it is the gift of God,
9 not of works, lest anyone should boast.

And then in his letter to the Galatians, he wrote that his entire relationship with Jesus and the new life of godliness came to him through faith.

Even his ability to live a crucified life came through faith.

Galatians 2:20
"I have been crucified with Christ; it is no longer I who live, but Christ lives in me; and the life which I now live in the flesh I live by faith in the Son of God, who loved me and gave Himself for me.

The Apostle Peter began his letter to believers by giving clear understanding regarding the process of purifying faith and its' value:

1 Peter 1:3-9
3 Blessed be the God and Father of our Lord Jesus Christ, who according to His abundant mercy has begotten us again to a living hope through the resurrection of Jesus Christ from the dead,
4 to an inheritance incorruptible and undefiled and that does not fade

away, reserved in heaven for you,
5 who are kept by the power of God through faith for salvation ready
to be revealed in the last time.
6 In this you greatly rejoice, though now for a little while, if need be,
you have been grieved by various trials,
7 that the genuineness of your faith, being much more precious than
gold that perishes, though it is tested by fire, may be found to praise,
honor, and glory at the revelation of Jesus Christ,
8 whom having not seen you love. Though now you do not see Him, yet
believing, you rejoice with joy inexpressible and full of glory,
9 receiving the end of your faith—the salvation of your souls.

In this passage Peter shows the important place our faith holds in our entire walk with God.

Most of us know the principles behind these precious verses. We know that our salvation comes from God's great heart of love and compassion. It comes as His free gift to us.

We call this love endowment "His Grace".

Grace is the unmerited favor of God.

But the way to appropriate, or take advantage of this marvelous gift, is by this small word "faith".

Faith is of highest importance to the Christian. For, all that we have and all that we can become in Christ, comes through the means of this amazing spiritual issue.

To the human mind faith is something intangible and outside of logic and reason. Therefore it is considered by many as frivolous and really unimportant.

To the spiritual mind faith is most valuable and is really the ultimate goal and attainment when it is placed in God.

John the beloved Apostle says:

1 John 5:4
For whatever is born of God overcomes the world. And this is the victory that has overcome the world—our faith.

The entire eleventh chapter of the Epistle to the Hebrews is dedicated to the establishment in clear understanding that all the Old Testament men of action and deliverance were being motivated and enabled by that simple spiritual ingredient called faith. And although it may seem to be exhaustive to read it, I am sure that by doing so the reader will realize the importance and relevancy of the subject matter for living in today's world.

Hebrews 11:4-40
4 By faith Abel offered to God a more excellent sacrifice than Cain, through which he obtained witness that he was righteous, God testifying of his gifts; and through it he being dead still speaks.
5 By faith Enoch was taken away so that he did not see death, "and was not found, because God had taken him"; for before he was taken he had this testimony, that he pleased God.
6 But without faith it is impossible to please Him, for he who comes to God must believe that He is, and that He is a rewarder of those who diligently seek Him.
7 By faith Noah, being divinely warned of things not yet seen, moved with godly fear, prepared an ark for the saving of his household, by which he condemned the world and became heir of the righteousness which is according to faith.
8 By faith Abraham obeyed when he was called to go out to the place which he would receive as an inheritance. And he went out, not knowing where he was going.
9 By faith he dwelt in the land of promise as in a foreign country, dwelling in tents with Isaac and Jacob, the heirs with him of the same promise;
10 for he waited for the city which has foundations, whose builder and maker is God.
11 By faith Sarah herself also received strength to conceive seed, and

she bore a child when she was past the age, because she judged Him faithful who had promised.
12 Therefore from one man, and him as good as dead, were born as many as the stars of the sky in multitude—innumerable as the sand which is by the seashore.
13 These all died in faith, not having received the promises, but having seen them afar off were assured of them, embraced them and confessed that they were strangers and pilgrims on the earth.
14 For those who say such things declare plainly that they seek a homeland.
15 And truly if they had called to mind that country from which they had come out, they would have had opportunity to return.
16 But now they desire a better, that is, a heavenly country. Therefore God is not ashamed to be called their God, for He has prepared a city for them.
17 By faith Abraham, when he was tested, offered up Isaac, and he who had received the promises offered up his only begotten son,
18 of whom it was said, "In Isaac your seed shall be called,"
19 concluding that God was able to raise him up, even from the dead, from which he also received him in a figurative sense.
20 By faith Isaac blessed Jacob and Esau concerning things to come.
21 By faith Jacob, when he was dying, blessed each of the sons of Joseph, and worshiped, leaning on the top of his staff.
22 By faith Joseph, when he was dying, made mention of the departure of the children of Israel, and gave instructions concerning his bones.
23 By faith Moses, when he was born, was hidden three months by his parents, because they saw he was a beautiful child; and they were not afraid of the king's command.
24 By faith Moses, when he became of age, refused to be called the son of Pharaoh's daughter,
25 choosing rather to suffer affliction with the people of God than to enjoy the passing pleasures of sin,
26 esteeming the reproach of Christ greater riches than the treasures in Egypt; for he looked to the reward.
27 By faith he forsook Egypt, not fearing the wrath of the king; for he endured as seeing Him who is invisible.
28 By faith he kept the Passover and the sprinkling of blood, lest he

who destroyed the firstborn should touch them.
29 By faith they passed through the Red Sea as by dry land, whereas the Egyptians, attempting to do so, were drowned.
30 By faith the walls of Jericho fell down after they were encircled for seven days.
31 By faith the harlot Rahab did not perish with those who did not believe, when she had received the spies with peace.
32 And what more shall I say? For the time would fail me to tell of Gideon and Barak and Samson and Jephthah, also of David and Samuel and the prophets:
33 who through faith subdued kingdoms, worked righteousness, obtained promises, stopped the mouths of lions,
34 quenched the violence of fire, escaped the edge of the sword, out of weakness were made strong, became valiant in battle, turned to flight the armies of the aliens.
35 Women received their dead raised to life again. And others were tortured, not accepting deliverance, that they might obtain a better resurrection.
36 Still others had trial of mockings and scourgings, yes, and of chains and imprisonment.
37 They were stoned, they were sawn in two, were tempted, were slain with the sword. They wandered about in sheepskins and goatskins, being destitute, afflicted, tormented—
38 of whom the world was not worthy. They wandered in deserts and mountains, in dens and caves of the earth.
39 And all these, having obtained a good testimony through faith, did not receive the promise,
40 God having provided something better for us, that they should not be made perfect apart from us.

First things first

The meaning of the word "faith"

In English its most basic meaning is: faith, complete confidence in someone or in something.

The Greek word translated as faith is: *"pistis"* meaning - faith, faithfulness, steadfastness.

It is extremely important to understand faith. But to do this we need to go to the Word of God, the source of faith, and draw from its deep streams.

Hebrews 11:1
Now faith is the substance of things hoped for, the evidence of things not seen.

Faith is a spiritual substance and it is spiritual evidence.

Hebrews 11:1 NIV
Now faith is being sure of what we hope for and certain of what we do not see.

According to this translation it is the ability to be sure and certain of what is not yet seen.

Therefore we can see that true faith is the enablement to be "sure" of what we are hoping to see and receive, and "certain" of things about which we do not yet have physical evidence.

We need to discover and enter into the foundational level of faith before trying to go on to other levels. Paul called this first level of faith: *"faith toward God"*.

Faith's direction

The first principle of faith is the direction of your faith. That is, what is your faith really focused on and resting in?

The Gospel demands that we believe *"in Jesus."*

Most of us do not place our faith in Him alone. We have a mixture of faith in other things.

* We believe in ourselves

This is manifested by only wanting a little bit of God's help. It is manifested specifically in great sadness and depression when we fail our own expectations.

This was the primary issue that caused Peter to fail. He had strong self confidence. He thought he could stand on his own strength.

* We believe in other people.

This is seen by the many people who quit when a leader falls short. They did not have their faith in God alone, but in the strength of other perceived leaders.

* We believe in our own understanding.

This is revealed through the struggle we go through when we are found in a situation that goes outside of what we understand God will do.

* We believe in religious systems.

One of the most common of all mixtures is when a person believes more in the belief structure or the religious institution than in the Lord Himself. When the institution does not come through for them, they become angry with God.

FAITH IN GOD

The story of Abraham and Sarah is found in *Genesis 12-25.* It tells how Abraham was given the promise of being the father of nations when his wife Sarah was in fact barren.

Abraham heard and believed the promise of God to him, and maintained a posture of faith in God for all the years of his life. His faith was tried both before and after Isaac was finally born. Yet

Abraham believed the promises because he believed God.

Paul the Apostle explained this process of Abraham's faith in the Book of Romans. Notice the powerful principle of faith in God at work in his teaching about the centrality of faith.

Romans 4:16-25
16 Therefore it is of faith that it might be according to grace, so that the promise might be sure to all the seed, not only to those who are of the law, but also to those who are of the faith of Abraham, who is the father of us all
17 (as it is written, "I have made you a father of many nations") in the presence of Him whom he believed—God, who gives life to the dead and calls those things which do not exist as though they did;
18 who, contrary to hope, in hope believed, so that he became the father of many nations, according to what was spoken, "So shall your descendants be."
19 And not being weak in faith, he did not consider his own body, already dead (since he was about a hundred years old), and the deadness of Sarah's womb.
20 He did not waver at the promise of God through unbelief, but was strengthened in faith, giving glory to God,
21 and being fully convinced that what He had promised He was also able to perform.
22 And therefore "it was accounted to him for righteousness."
23 Now it was not written for his sake alone that it was imputed to him,
24 but also for us. It shall be imputed to us who believe in Him who raised up Jesus our Lord from the dead,
25 who was delivered up because of our offenses, and was raised because of our justification.

Faith in God Himself is the greatest kind of faith we can have. It is the faith that Abraham possessed. He was able to believe God when nothing else made any sense to him. He was able to believe God even though he was aware of his and Sarah's own weaknesses.

It was this basic kind of faith that God rewarded Abraham for.

HOW DOES FAITH OPERATE IN US?

Romans 10:8-10
8 But what does it say? "The word is near you, in your mouth and in your heart" (that is, the word of faith which we preach):
9 that if you confess with your mouth the Lord Jesus and believe in your heart that God has raised Him from the dead, you will be saved.
10 For with the heart one believes unto righteousness, and with the mouth confession is made unto salvation.

Verse 17
So then faith comes by hearing, and hearing by the word of God.

God's Word reveals that placing ourselves under the power of His Word (whether through reading, listening to preaching and teaching, or studying Scripture) releases the "word of faith" in our hearts. As we yield to it and simply begin to confess with our mouths and believe in our hearts, we are saved, delivered and changed.

The word of faith is found in the Word of God. It is the voice of the Spirit of God that speaks the word of faith into our hearts.

Every other level of faith springs from that simple foundational faith experience.

UNBELIEF

Probably the most difficult thing to look at squarely is our own unbelief.

What is unbelief? And how do we get rid of it?

Unbelief is the refusal to believe what God has said.

2 Corinthians 10:3-5 reveals that the stronghold of the enemy is in fact most of the time our own thinking process.

3 For though we walk in the flesh, we do not war according to the flesh.
4 For the weapons of our warfare are not carnal but mighty in God for pulling down strongholds,
5 casting down arguments and every high thing that exalts itself against the knowledge of God, bringing every thought into captivity to the obedience of Christ,

Satan attacks us through our minds.

Most unbelief originates in the mind and is accepted in the heart.

This is why faith speaks in the heart. (*Romans 10:9-10*)

There is also an unbelieving heart.

Hebrews 3:12
Beware, brethren, lest there be in any of you an evil heart of unbelief in departing from the living God;

This kind of unbelief is very hard to reason with.

Honest unbelief can be convinced.

The Lord demonstrates patience with honest unbelief as he did in the case of Thomas' doubts after the resurrection.

John 20:24-28
24 Now Thomas, called the Twin, one of the twelve, was not with them when Jesus came.
25 The other disciples therefore said to him, "We have seen the Lord." So he said to them, "Unless I see in His hands the print of the nails, and put my finger into the print of the nails, and put my hand into His side, I will not believe."
26 And after eight days His disciples were again inside, and Thomas with them. Jesus came, the doors being shut, and stood in the midst, and said, "Peace to you!"

27 Then He said to Thomas, "Reach your finger here, and look at My hands; and reach your hand here, and put it into My side. Do not be unbelieving, but believing."
28 And Thomas answered and said to Him, "My Lord and my God!"

Yet in many other Biblical cases, unbelief solidified even when miracles were performed by Jesus.

When Jesus cast demons out, the unbelieving heart attributed the power to demons.

Matthew 9:33-34
33 And when the demon was cast out, the mute spoke. And the multitudes marveled, saying, "It was never seen like this in Israel!"
34 But the Pharisees said, "He casts out demons by the ruler of the demons."

When Jesus healed the withered hand these same people began their plot to kill Him.

Matthew 12:13-14
13 Then He said to the man, "Stretch out your hand." And he stretched it out, and it was restored as whole as the other.
14 Then the Pharisees went out and plotted against Him, how they might destroy Him.

Notice in these examples that faith and unbelief were provoked by the same circumstance.

The same thing happened when Jesus raised Lazarus. A large crowd believed in Jesus and a large crowd ran to tell the leaders:

John 11:45-46
45 Then many of the Jews who had come to Mary, and had seen the things Jesus did, believed in Him.
46 But some of them went away to the Pharisees and told them the things Jesus did.

In this incident the scripture reveals what was really happening. Their unbelief was caused by their desire to cling to their earthly position.

John 11:46-48
46 But some of them went away to the Pharisees and told them the things Jesus did.
47 Then the chief priests and the Pharisees gathered a council and said, "What shall we do? For this Man works many signs.
48 "If we let Him alone like this, everyone will believe in Him, and the Romans will come and take away both our place and nation."

It was clear that the motive of their hearts was to cling to their position rather than believe in Jesus. This is the *"evil heart of unbelief."*

Miracles do not always cause people to believe. If they are honestly doubtful, yes, miracles will help them believe, but most are not honestly doubtful.

Jesus gave us a strong insight into why people do not believe.

John 12:37-43
37 But although He had done so many signs before them, they did not believe in Him,
38 that the word of Isaiah the prophet might be fulfilled, which he spoke:

> *"Lord, who has believed our report?*
> *And to whom has the arm of the LORD been revealed?"*

39 Therefore they could not believe, because Isaiah said again:

40 "He has blinded their eyes and hardened their hearts,
Lest they should see with their eyes,
Lest they should understand with their hearts and turn,
So that I should heal them."

41 These things Isaiah said when he saw His glory and spoke of Him.

42 Nevertheless even among the rulers many believed in Him, but because of the Pharisees they did not confess Him, lest they should be put out of the synagogue;
43 for they loved the praise of men more than the praise of God.

Scripture reveals that men do not believe many times because they want to retain their present status and that they love each others praises more than the praise of God.

It is why our relationships can be the biggest hindrance to believing fully in God.

Faith in God comes as a result of the Holy Spirits' power to quicken the Word of God, or bring it to life in you.

Our part is to believe and confess it. Believing is partly because of evidence we are familiar with, and partly by the decision to accept it as true. As long as you don't make the decision to believe, you stay in a position of unbelief. You will stay in that unsure position until you decide to believe God's record and testimony.

True saving faith begins by believing in Jesus Christ alone!

This first dimension of faith will support the entire walk of faith, and carry it into fullness.

Faith in God's Word

The only place for faith to anchor itself is in God Himself.

True saving faith comes from the revelation that Jesus Christ is the Son of God.

The power of the Blood of Jesus is of no avail to you unless you are sure that He is the Son of God.

And God's Word is of no real value to you unless you believe in God Himself. Only then can you have faith in His Word.

Romans 10:17
So then faith comes by hearing, and hearing by the word of God.

The Word of God produces faith in God, which in turn establishes faith in His Word and acts as light in our walk in the Spirit.

When the Apostle Paul wanted to correct the error of the Galatian Christians who had been deceived into thinking that they were made perfect by the works of the Law, he asked them a rhetorical question:

Galatians 3:1-3
1 O foolish Galatians! Who has bewitched you that you should not obey the truth, before whose eyes Jesus Christ was clearly portrayed among you as crucified?
2 This only I want to learn from you: Did you receive the Spirit by the works of the law, or by the hearing of faith?
3 Are you so foolish? Having begun in the Spirit, are you now being made perfect by the flesh?

The Apostle makes it very clear that our faith is the issue that opens the door to all the treasures of the Holy Spirit. Faith begins with our salvation but it is also the means to every gift of God and every ministry of the Holy Spirit.

It can be clearly affirmed therefore that the walk of the Spirit is a walk of faith.

Questions to ponder:

1. How important is faith to you?

2. Do you take pride in being hard to convince and cynical?

3. Is your faith in God pure, or is it mixed with faith in religious systems and their leaders?

4. If the Word of God is the source of faith, do you give time and energy to the Word?

5 Do you "plow the soil" of your heart so that faith can have its full strength to develop?

Chapter 10
Love

The greatest commandment Jesus gave to His disciples was given to them on His last personal ministry time with them, The Last Supper.

After sharing the Passover meal and the bread and wine of the first Communion, with close eye contact across the table, He gave them this command.

It was to be a primary part of all their lives and service. It was to be their mark of identity, the essence of who they were.

John 13:34-35
"A new commandment I give to you, that you love one another; as I have loved you, that you also love one another.
35 "By this all will know that you are My disciples, if you have love for one another."

Notice that Jesus told them it was *"a new commandment."* No one had ever been asked to live this way before.

It was to be directed to *"one another."* It had a set group of people in mind.

It was qualified by the explanation *"as I have loved you."* Which made plain the kind and quality of the love being commanded.

And then it was repeated again to emphasize it dramatically.

He finished by telling them that their love for one another would be the sign of authenticity upon the true disciples of Jesus the world over.

The command of Jesus to His first disciples has never changed. It is still foundational to the life and function of all true disciples today.

Love had been so integral a part of the life of the Church that in his ministry to the Gentiles, the Apostle Paul spoke of it as the means to fulfill all the rest of God's commandments.

In his letter to Timothy, the Apostle says:

1 Timothy 1:5-6
5 Now the purpose of the commandment is love from a pure heart, from a good conscience, and from sincere faith,
6 from which some, having strayed, have turned aside to idle talk,

Love has been a central theme of God's commandments from ancient times.

The first commandment

When Jesus was asked about his opinion regarding the most important commandment of all, He gave us the following:

Matthew 22:37-40
Jesus said to him," "You shall love the LORD your God with all your heart, with all your soul, and with all your mind."
38 "This is the first and great commandment.
39 "And the second is like it: "You shall love your neighbor as yourself."
40 "On these two commandments hang all the Law and the Prophets."

These two commandments were quoted from the Old Testament books of Moses. The first is found in:

Deuteronomy 6:4-5
4 "Hear, O Israel: The LORD our God, the LORD is one!
5 "You shall love the LORD your God with all your heart, with all your soul, and with all your strength."

The second is from:

Leviticus 19:18
"You shall not take vengeance, nor bear any grudge against the children of your people, but you shall love your neighbor as yourself: I am the LORD."

Jesus placed these two commandments first in order of importance, and then in their order of function and enablement.

Loving the Lord

Loving the Lord comes from first believing and receiving His love toward us. We have to receive His love and "abide" in it in order to return it to Him.

1 John 4: 16
And we have known and believed the love that God has for us. God is love, and he who abides in love abides in God, and God in him.

And *verse 19: "We love Him because He first loved us."*

On another occasion, Jesus conversed with a lawyer who was questioning Him about the "first" commandment. This time the lawyer repeated from Leviticus with an additional insight Jesus agreed to:

Luke 10:25-28
And behold, a certain lawyer stood up and tested Him, saying, "Teacher, what shall I do to inherit eternal life?"
26 He said to him, "What is written in the law? What is your reading of it?"
27 So he answered and said," "You shall love the LORD your God with all your heart, with all your soul, with all your strength, and with all your mind," and "your neighbor as yourself.'"
28 And He said to him, "You have answered rightly; do this and you will live."

God's own command: We are to love Him with all -

* our heart

* our soul

* our strength

* our mind

Loving each other

As we love God, we are enabled to fulfill the second commandment which is to love our neighbor.

The Apostle Paul commented on this when explaining the error of using personal rights in a way that could cause hurt to others. He showed the connection to love by first dealing with personal debts to the brethren and then repeating different commandments given by God from Mount Sinai:

Romans 13:8-10
Owe no one anything except to love one another, for he who loves another has fulfilled the law.
9 For the commandments, "You shall not commit adultery," "You shall not murder," "You shall not steal," "You shall not bear false witness," "You shall not covet," and if there is any other commandment, are all summed up in this saying, namely, "You shall love your neighbor as yourself."
10 Love does no harm to a neighbor; therefore love is the fulfillment of the law.

Jesus came to reveal the true nature of the Father. By taking on human form and declaring through word and deed the fullness of His love, He unveiled the true image of God that man had never seen before. As He walked in open relationship with His disciples, they began to experience the most wonderful thing of all. It had to be given to them little by little, day by day, for they did not know that God is love.

As a result, Love became the essence of the ministry of the early Church. It had been the primary characteristic of the life of Jesus.

The Apostle John wrote about this experience:

1 John 1:1-2
That which was from the beginning, which we have heard, which we have seen with our eyes, which we have looked upon, and our hands have handled, concerning the Word of life-
2 the life was manifested, and we have seen, and bear witness, and declare to you that eternal life which was with the Father and was manifested to us.

As a result of Jesus' life lived among them, the Disciples understood that His commandments were also life-giving to those who would obey them by believing in them.

They began to believe in God's love and to walk in its assurance. Even though they had failed miserably, they believed in His love for them. They remained sure of His forgiveness and experienced transformation as they believed Him. His love did dwell in them and it enabled them to love as He had commanded.

Each new step of faith brought new experiences of God's love. Each new dimension of obedience to love brought new dimensions of His presence and blessing. It became so powerful that love became the core of their message. The Apostle John wrote:

1 John 4:7-11
Beloved, let us love one another, for love is of God; and everyone who loves is born of God and knows God.
8 He who does not love does not know God, for God is love.
9 In this the love of God was manifested toward us, that God has sent His only begotten Son into the world, that we might live through Him.
10 In this is love, not that we loved God, but that He loved us and sent His Son to be the propitiation for our sins.
11 Beloved, if God so loved us, we also ought to love one another.

John found out that living in God's love delivered them from their fears and gave them boldness.

Verses 16-18
16 And we have known and believed the love that God has for us. God is love, and he who abides in love abides in God, and God in him.
17 Love has been perfected among us in this: that we may have boldness in the day of judgment; because as He is, so are we in this world.
18 There is no fear in love; but perfect love casts out fear, because fear involves torment. But he who fears has not been made perfect in love.

Love out of a pure heart

There are three Greek words that are translated "love" in modern American vernacular.

One is the word *"eros"* from where we get our animal love concept. You can see this word in the English word "erotic." It speaks of heightened sexual passion.

The Greek word *"phileo"* speaks of human affection in terms of fondness and family relationships. It is used many times in the Bible to speak of the inter-relationship between the brethren. The American city Philadelphia, "the city of brotherly love", is named after this Greek concept.

Finally, the Greek word *"agape"* meaning affection, benevolence, and love, is the word used to denote a love of covenant and spiritual commitment. This is the love commanded by the Bible between disciples of Jesus. However, Jesus redefined this word for believers world over.

Human language can only express human experiences. Jesus introduced a new level of human experience with his loving relationship to His disciples. Therefore, when He gave them the great commandment regarding "agape" love, He added His relationship with them as the definition of what He was commanding them:

John 13:34
"A new commandment I give to you, that you love one another; as I have loved you, that you also love one another."

The first platform for loving in this new dimension of love is a *"pure heart."*

Purity means not diluted or contaminated with any foreign substance.

The *"heart"* is that part of us that contains the fullness of our personality.

The word "heart" is used more than 900 times in the Bible, and only once mentioned as a physical body organ. In all the other times, it is mentioned in the spiritual sense meaning the center of the mind, will, and emotions.

Because the human being is made up of spiritual parts as well as physical, it is difficult to explain the portions of our being that the Bible talks about. The parts make the whole and without any part there is no whole person. The heart is the combination of the mind, will, and emotions. All these parts together create the heart.

By this we can see that to obtain purity of heart we must deal with each of these three.

1. Our minds must be purified

2. Our wills must be purified

3. Our emotions must be purified

Otherwise they will tend to contaminate our hearts.

This explains why Jesus taught that most sin proceeds out of man's heart.

In His response to the accusation that by not washing their hands the Disciples had contaminated themselves, He replied:

Matthew 15:17-20
"Do you not yet understand that whatever enters the mouth goes into the stomach and is eliminated?
18 "But those things which proceed out of the mouth come from the heart, and they defile a man.
19 "For out of the heart proceed evil thoughts, murders, adulteries, fornications, thefts, false witness, blasphemies.
20 "These are the things which defile a man, but to eat with unwashed hands does not defile a man."

Jesus taught that sinfulness begins in the heart of man. His actions of sinfulness are the result of the sin sickness living in him.

The Old Testament bears witness:

Jeremiah 17:9
> *The heart is deceitful above all things,*
> *And desperately wicked;*
> *Who can know it?*

For this reason the pure heart is the first and foremost platform for God's love to be expressed to us and through us.

Finally, the real measure of our life in God, our value in service, and our anointing, is found in the dimension of love we live in. The Apostle Paul wrote:

1 Corinthians 13:1-13
Though I speak with the tongues of men and of angels, but have not love, I have become sounding brass or a clanging cymbal.
2 And though I have the gift of prophecy, and understand all mysteries and all knowledge, and though I have all faith, so that I could remove mountains, but have not love, I am nothing.
3 And though I bestow all my goods to feed the poor, and though I give

my body to be burned, but have not love, it profits me nothing.
4 Love suffers long and is kind; love does not envy; love does not
parade itself, is not puffed up;
5 does not behave rudely, does not seek its own, is not provoked, thinks
no evil;
6 does not rejoice in iniquity, but rejoices in the truth;
7 bears all things, believes all things, hopes all things, endures all
things.
8 Love never fails. But whether there are prophecies, they will fail;
whether there are tongues, they will cease; whether there is
knowledge, it will vanish away.
9 For we know in part and we prophesy in part.
10 But when that which is perfect has come, then that which is in part
will be done away.
11 When I was a child, I spoke as a child, I understood as a child, I
thought as a child; but when I became a man, I put away childish
things.
12 For now we see in a mirror, dimly, but then face to face. Now I
know in part, but then I shall know just as I also am known.
13 And now abide faith, hope, love, these three; but the greatest of
these is love.

Love is the basic characteristic of the heart of God expressed in Jesus' life and ministry. It was His first Disciples' highest ideal.

Jesus commanded His first Disciples to love each other, and He commanded that they love each other just as He had loved them.

It is the purifying of our hearts that enables love to become powerful. It is the mixture of agendas, purposes and desires that causes our hearts to receive and send a diluted and distorted picture of God's love.

We must examine our hearts to see if God's love has a pure container for its fullest expression. If we find that our hearts lack purity then its' purification must become our major issue of prayer and pursuit. The cleansing of our hearts is imperative.

Love ministered to and from each disciple is the main issue.

A pure heart is the first platform from which our lives can present God's love back to Him and to each other.

If that platform is impure with personal motives and carnal desires, the love that comes through it becomes tainted and constrained.

When we are cleansed from sin, we live in "confidence," the highest level of faith.

1 John 3:18-23
My little children, let us not love in word or in tongue, but in deed and in truth.
19 And by this we know that we are of the truth, and shall assure our hearts before Him.
20 For if our heart condemns us, God is greater than our heart, and knows all things.
21 Beloved, if our heart does not condemn us, we have confidence toward God.
22 And whatever we ask we receive from Him, because we keep His commandments and do those things that are pleasing in His sight.
23 And this is His commandment: that we should believe on the name of His Son Jesus Christ and love one another, as He gave us commandment.

HOW DO WE GET STARTED?

There are two dimensions of love that are commanded to the believer.

The first is the *"phileo"* love for all the brethren. The second is the higher level *"agape"* love commanded between disciples. In Peter's command to the believers in persecution he used both terms in the same sentence.

1 Peter 1:22
"Since you have purified your souls in obeying the truth through the Spirit in sincere love of the brethren, love one another fervently with a pure heart,"

He shows that "*sincere love of the brethren* " - (philadelphia) was to be followed up with fervent "*love*" (agape) toward "*one another*."

The affection existing between the fellowship of believers was to be fanned into the committed love of covenant among those in close relationship.

The issue of increasing levels of love is constant in most of the Epistles.

The Apostle Paul also uses the terms side by side: (Notice the parenthesis for Greek terms used.)

1 Thessalonians 4:9-10
9 But concerning brotherly love (philadelphia) you have no need that I should write to you, for you yourselves are taught by God to love (agapao) one another;
10 and indeed you do so toward all the brethren who are in all Macedonia. But we urge you, brethren, that you increase more and more;

In his Philippian letter, the Apostle Paul shows the same need to increase love through knowledge and discernment, with the promise of the rewards of fruitfulness:

Philippians 1:9-11
9 And this I pray, that your love may abound still more and more in knowledge and all discernment,
10 that you may approve the things that are excellent, that you may be sincere and without offense till the day of Christ,
11 being filled with the fruits of righteousness which are by Jesus Christ, to the glory and praise of God.

Paul's prayer for the Ephesians was very similar:

Ephesians 3:17-19
17 "that Christ may dwell in your hearts through faith; that you, being rooted and grounded in love,
18 may be able to comprehend with all the saints what is the width and length and depth and height—
19 to know the love of Christ which passes knowledge; that you may be filled with all the fullness of God."

He continued in the next chapter including attitudes and actions that will encourage love:

Chapter 4:31-5:2
31 "Let all bitterness, wrath, anger, clamor, and evil speaking be put away from you, with all malice.
32 And be kind to one another, tenderhearted, forgiving one another, just as God in Christ forgave you."

Chapter 5
1 "Therefore be imitators of God as dear children.
2 And walk in love, as Christ also has loved us and given Himself for us, an offering and a sacrifice to God for a sweet-smelling aroma.

He becomes very specific about issues that increase and hinder love in his letter to the Colossians:

Colossians 3:12-14
12 "Therefore, as the elect of God, holy and beloved, put on tender mercies, kindness, humility, meekness, longsuffering;
13 bearing with one another, and forgiving one another, if anyone has a complaint against another; even as Christ forgave you, so you also must do.
14 But above all these things put on love, which is the bond of perfection."

Here again, walking and living in love is called the highest form of Christian living.

The Apostle John comes from the other direction:

1 John 3:14-19
14 "We know that we have passed from death to life, because we love the brethren. He who does not love his brother abides in death.
15 Whoever hates his brother is a murderer, and you know that no murderer has eternal life abiding in him.
16 By this we know love, because He laid down His life for us. And we also ought to lay down our lives for the brethren.
17 But whoever has this world's goods, and sees his brother in need, and shuts up his heart from him, how does the love of God abide in him?
18 My little children, let us not love in word or in tongue, but in deed and in truth.
19 And by this we know that we are of the truth, and shall assure our hearts before Him."

Verses 23-24
23 "And this is His commandment: that we should believe on the name of His Son Jesus Christ and love one another, as He gave us commandment.
24 Now he who keeps His commandments abides in Him, and He in him. And by this we know that He abides in us, by the Spirit whom He has given us."

Chapter 4:7-11
7 "Beloved, let us love one another, for love is of God; and everyone who loves is born of God and knows God.
8 He who does not love does not know God, for God is love.
9 In this the love of God was manifested toward us, that God has sent His only begotten Son into the world, that we might live through Him.
10 In this is love, not that we loved God, but that He loved us and sent His Son to be the propitiation for our sins.
11 Beloved, if God so loved us, we also ought to love one another."

According to John's writings, those who hate their brothers in the Lord, and those who do not continually love, are not true Disciples.

Those who do not love do not know God in truth.

God's love is given to us as a stewardship relationship with the Body.

It must be allowed to rule our lives. It is the essence of the Kingdom of God. It does not have to be faked, or drummed up. Love is given to us by the Holy Spirit. It is part of the life of Jesus that comes to dwell in our hearts at conversion.

Any attitude or practice that is allowed to rule instead must be brought under the rulership of the Holy Spirit.

This is no small matter. Love is the very substance and nature of the Holy Spirit which has been given to us. He has called us to this very hope, that we could glorify God and obtain his own righteousness.

Romans 5:5
5 "Now hope does not disappoint, because the love of God has been poured out in our hearts by the Holy Spirit who was given to us."

If it has been poured out in our hearts, we must then acknowledge it and allow for love to be the center of our lives.

Philemon 5-6
5 "hearing of your love and faith which you have toward the Lord Jesus and toward all the saints,
6 that the sharing of your faith may become effective by the acknowledgment of every good thing which is in you in Christ Jesus."

The Apostle John sums it all up by writing:

1 John 2:23-24
23 "And this is His commandment: that we should believe on the name of His Son Jesus Christ and love one another, as He have us commandment.

24 Now he who keeps His commandments abides in Him, and He in him. And by this we know that He abides in us, by the Spirit whom He has given us."

To live and walk in the power of the Holy Spirit we must obey his commandments to love one another. His presence permeates and inspires that love.

To live outside of this powerful provision and commandment of God is to leave His heart and personality out of all that we do and all we become in Him.

Walking in the Spirit is a walk of love, in love with God, and extending that love to "*one another.*"

Questions to ponder:

1. How do you define your love for God?

2. Do you love Him as He has clearly commanded?

3. Do you have a group of disciples within the Body that you love?

4. How many disciples do you love?

5. Are you satisfied with your love relationship with God?

6. Are you satisfied with your love relationship with your "one another" group?

Chapter 11
Rest

Matthew 11:25-30
25 At that time Jesus answered and said, "I thank You, Father, Lord of heaven and earth, that You have hidden these things from the wise and prudent and have revealed them to babes.
26 "Even so, Father, for so it seemed good in Your sight.
27 "All things have been delivered to Me by My Father, and no one knows the Son except the Father. Nor does anyone know the Father except the Son, and the one to whom the Son wills to reveal Him.
28 "Come to Me, all you who labor and are heavy laden, and I will give you rest.
29 "Take My yoke upon you and learn from Me, for I am gentle and lowly in heart, and you will find rest for your souls.
30 "For My yoke is easy and My burden is light."

To the Gentile Christian who is not versed in Old Testament principles, the meaning of these verses can be difficult.

"Rest" to most of us means to take a little time of relaxation and repose so that our natural strength can be replenished. However, this was not what Jesus was talking to His Disciples about. It was the Rest of the Holy Spirit. This important Biblical concept of Rest should be understood by everyone who follows Jesus.

For the believer, God's Rest is extremely important. Because, as we begin to work toward the accomplishment of the Kingdom of God - by serving, giving, praying and worshiping, if we do not understand Jesus as our Rest we will return to the idea of "works unto salvation." Or, we will end up "striving" rather than walking in the Spirit.

It is important to look closely at the Old Testament concept of Rest and then study the New Testament revelation of its´ hidden meaning.

Then we can apply the principles to our own lives today.

There are many words used in the Old Testament that are translated 'rest' in our modern Bibles. Some of the more important are:

* *The rest* - those portions remaining, such as the rest of the people, or the rest of the cattle.

* *rest* - a settling down, such as a relaxation or taking physical rest.

* *rest* - a place of rest, or a haven.

* *rest* - a cessation.

It is the Hebrew words "*Shabbathon*" and "*Menuchah*", meaning "cessation", and a "place of rest" that we need to look at more closely.

The word "Sabbath" (*"Shabbathon")*, means cessation, or to cease. It is most commonly referred to as "the Sabbath" or seventh day.

For this reason many believe it means "seventh", but it doesn't, it simply refers to the command of God regarding the seventh day.

Menuchah, refers to a "place where you rest". This is also important, for rest is accomplished best in the place of rest.

The picture is seen most clearly in God's promise to Israel while they were in Egypt.

They were in a place of slavery, and their labor was intense.

God's deliverance from that bondage was to take them out of the kingdom of bondage, and into relationship with Himself. They were to come first to Him. Then He would give them a place where rest could be accomplished in its completeness.

He was Himself their resting place first in the wilderness, then

Canaan. The land of promise, Canaan, was where this resting relationship would be accomplished in its fullness.

The Red Sea was the place of their deliverance from the place of bondage.

The River Jordan was their entrance into a place of Resting.

The place of rest did not mean that they would not be active.

Their rest was never inactivity. However, it was a drastic change in the way they carried out their activities. In fact, they would have to fight in order to conquer the enemies that occupied their resting place. And so it is today.

The first commandments concerning *Shabbathon*, or "the Sabbaths" is found in the Book of Exodus:

Exodus 20:8-11
8 "Remember the Sabbath day, to keep it holy.
9 Six days you shall labor and do all your work,
10 but the seventh day is the Sabbath of the LORD your God. In it you shall do no work: you, nor your son, nor your daughter, nor your male servant, nor your female servant, nor your cattle, nor your stranger who is within your gates.
11 For in six days the LORD made the heavens and the earth, the sea, and all that is in them, and rested the seventh day. Therefore the LORD blessed the Sabbath day and hallowed it.

This is the fourth commandment given by the Lord to the people of Israel as they stood before Mount Sinai after crossing the Red Sea.

It is one of the life principles of Old Testament Law.

Because there was no English word to fit it exactly, the translators transliterated the Hebrew word *"Shabbathon"* and called it *"Sabbath"* so that we would understand.

But now, centuries later, the word "Sabbath" has become part of our own language, yet without the understanding of the original meaning. As a result many readers do not fully understand God's intention as they read, but simply hold to the commonly held understanding of the day.

The commandment clearly refers back to God's own rest, and commands that we do the same. But what was it that God did to "Sabbath", (or Rest)?

There are some interesting things to note about the first Sabbath, or "*shabbathon*".

The Bibles says:

Genesis 2:1-1
1 Thus the heavens and the earth, and all the host of them, were finished.
2 And on the seventh day God ended His work which He had done, and He rested on the seventh day from all His work which He had done.

Notice that the seventh day was the only day of creation that was not officially ended.

Scripture reveals what God was doing as he rested, or "Sabbathed" -

Genesis 3:8
And they heard the sound of the LORD God walking in the garden in the cool of the day, and Adam and his wife hid themselves from the presence of the LORD God among the trees of the garden.

God's form of rest was to come down and walk in His creation, and relate in fellowship with the man and woman of His love.

Rest, to God, was fellowship and enjoyment of what He had made.

This is no doubt why Jesus said, *"Come unto me ... and you shall find rest for your souls.*

The flow of God's presence upon our lives is the only thing that can really bring us rest and refreshing.

What about the command to do no work?

Look at the other commandments concerning the Sabbath:

Days

* There was the Shabbat of the seventh day. *Exodus 20:8* we have already read.

Weeks

* There were the Shabbat weeks during the year. They were the weeks of:

Passover
Pentecost
Trumpets
Tabernacles

These commandments of "Shabbat" days and their special weeks were also called "Holy Days". It is where we get the concept of "holidays".

Years

The seventh year

Leviticus 25:3-4
3 Six years you shall sow your field, and six years you shall prune your vineyard, and gather its fruit;
4 'but in the seventh year there shall be a sabbath of solemn rest for the land, a sabbath to the LORD. You shall neither sow your field nor prune your vineyard.

The year of Jubilee

Leviticus 25:10-12
10 'And you shall consecrate the fiftieth year, and proclaim liberty throughout all the land to all its inhabitants. It shall be a Jubilee for you; and each of you shall return to his possession, and each of you shall return to his family.
11 'That fiftieth year shall be a Jubilee to you; in it you shall neither sow nor reap what grows of its own accord, nor gather the grapes of your untended vine.
12 'For it is the Jubilee; it shall be holy to you; you shall eat its produce from the field.

In each of these commandments to "rest" we find an important principle of what God gives to us when we come to Him correctly.

On the Seventh day, and all other Sabbath days, the people were to cease from all activity while the priest offered the correct sacrifices for their sin and salvation.

This reveals clearly that the first rest is the accomplishment of our redemption by Jesus alone in the Heavenly Tabernacle, hidden from natural view, but believed on though faith.

Salvation is the work we can never accomplish ourselves. God commands us to "rest" while He does it for us. We can only receive it as a gift of Grace. And we "rest in our salvation" through faith in Him.

We cease from our labors to save ourselves and enter into His Rest of fellowship and communion because He has saved us.

Passover - teaches us to feast on the Lamb while God covers our sin and protects us from death, knowing that He will lead us out of the place of bondage.

Pentecost - teaches that we must receive and enter into the outpouring of the Holy Spirit, and the first fruits of righteousness that the Spirit brings to us, by resting in His provision and trusting only in Him.

Isaiah 28:11-12
For with stammering lips and another tongue He will speak to this people,
To whom He said, "This is the rest with which You may cause the weary to rest," And, "This is the refreshing"; Yet they would not hear.

This prophesy was fulfilled at the feast of Pentecost in Jerusalem soon after Jesus was resurrected and ascended into heaven.

Trumpets - speaks of the coming of the Lord and all His great acts upon the earth. We can relax knowing that we have been saved by grace, and that He is in control in spite of what Satan tries to tell us.

Tabernacles - the time when Jews were commanded to live once again in make shift houses and tents, was to renew the understanding that we do not live permanently in this world, but look for an eternal home in heaven.

This world is not our home. We have a mansion in Father's House. We rest in that truth!

All these Shabbats, or "Sabbaths" were, as Paul called them, shadows of what would come when Jesus fulfilled it all.

Colossians 2:16-17
16 So let no one judge you in food or in drink, or regarding a festival or a new moon or sabbaths,
17 which are a shadow of things to come, but the substance is of Christ.

This explains why Jesus corrected His Disciples when they would begin to get upset with fear or unbelief. It went against the principle of Resting in faith.

He wanted them to know that they could walk assuredly and without panic or fear when they obeyed His Word in faith.

Scriptural example revealed that God's grace would provide for them in every instance of faithful obedience.

Jesus had said:
John 14:1
"Let not your heart be troubled; you believe in God, believe also in Me.

Verse 27
"Peace I leave with you, My peace I give to you; not as the world gives do I give to you. Let not your heart be troubled, neither let it be afraid.

You see, most of our refusing to draw near and enter into relationship, blessing, and rest in our own labors, comes from the problem of fear and unbelief.

When I fear, I am believing that something outside of God's control will happen to me.

Unbelief causes me to take my life into my own hands and go my own way. Because, for whatever reason, I don't believe I can trust God to work things the way He has promised.

The writer of Hebrews warned the Jewish believers of the time to remember their own natural history so they would enter into God's promises fully:

Hebrews 3:12-4:11
12 Beware, brethren, lest there be in any of you an evil heart of unbelief in departing from the living God;
13 but exhort one another daily, while it is called "Today," lest any of you be hardened through the deceitfulness of sin.
14 For we have become partakers of Christ if we hold the beginning of our confidence steadfast to the end,
15 while it is said: "Today, if you will hear His voice, Do not harden your hearts as in the rebellion."

16 For who, having heard, rebelled? Indeed, was it not all who came out of Egypt, led by Moses?
17 Now with whom was He angry forty years? Was it not with those who sinned, whose corpses fell in the wilderness?
18 And to whom did He swear that they would not enter His rest, but to those who did not obey?
19 So we see that they could not enter in because of unbelief.
1 Therefore, since a promise remains of entering His rest, let us fear lest any of you seem to have come short of it.
2 For indeed the gospel was preached to us as well as to them; but the word which they heard did not profit them, not being mixed with faith in those who heard it.
3 For we who have believed do enter that rest, as He has said: "So I swore in My wrath, 'They shall not enter My rest,'" although the works were finished from the foundation of the world.
4 For He has spoken in a certain place of the seventh day in this way: "And God rested on the seventh day from all His works";
5 and again in this place: "They shall not enter My rest."
6 Since therefore it remains that some must enter it, and those to whom it was first preached did not enter because of disobedience,
7 again He designates a certain day, saying in David, "Today," after such a long time, as it has been said: "Today, if you will hear His voice, Do not harden your hearts."
8 For if Joshua had given them rest, then He would not afterward have spoken of another day.
9 There remains therefore a rest for the people of God.
10 For he who has entered His rest has himself also ceased from his works as God did from His.
11 Let us therefore be diligent to enter that rest, lest anyone fall according to the same example of disobedience.

There is rest in God.

* Rest is an attitude of confidence in the middle of trials.

* Rest is confidence that God will always supply.

* Rest is casting your care upon Him

* Rest is knowing that you are accepted by God.

* Rest is forgiving and being forgiven.

* Rest is obeying the Spirit and walking God's way.

* Rest is serving Him because we love Him, not to attain His love.

* Rest is working in the works of God.

* Rest is drawing deeply from His Presence, enjoying the shelter of His power over you and yours.

* **Rest is Jesus Himself. He is our Sabbath.**

There is godly wisdom in honoring special days unto the Lord regularly:

The seventh day rest

In regard to the weekly day of rest, Jesus said:

Mark 2:27-28
27 And He said to them, "The Sabbath was made for man, and not man for the Sabbath.
28 "Therefore the Son of Man is also Lord of the Sabbath."

Notice what Jesus did not say:

He did not say that we didn't need the "Sabbath" anymore.

He did not say that this law was one that did not need to be observed anymore.

He instructed His Disciples concerning the Written Law:

Matthew 5:19
"Whoever therefore breaks one of the least of these commandments, and teaches men so, shall be called least in the kingdom of heaven; but whoever does and teaches them, he shall be called great in the kingdom of heaven.

Concerning the seventh day He said:

He said: *"The Sabbath was made for man, and not man for the Sabbath."*

The wisdom of the Law of God is still in effect. Man needs to break the rhythm of life and return to the Peace and Rest of the Lord. If he doesn't, he will find it difficult to walk in The Spirit.

That is why the Church, especially today when people are so very busy, calls people to come together and worship God on Sundays.

Unfortunately, most do not understand why, and therefore regard the "sabbath day" fulfilled with short services and the rest of the day is dedicated to play.

The commandment concerning the seventh day was not to make it holy, but *to "keep it holy"*.

Exodus 20:8-11
8 "Remember the Sabbath day, to keep it holy.
9 Six days you shall labor and do all your work,
10 but the seventh day is the Sabbath of the LORD your God. In it you shall do no work: you, nor your son, nor your daughter, nor your male servant, nor your female servant, nor your cattle, nor your stranger who is within your gates.
11 For in six days the LORD made the heavens and the earth, the sea, and all that is in them, and rested the seventh day. Therefore the LORD blessed the Sabbath day and hallowed it.

If we take just a few moments to meditate about the value of dedicating one day a week to focus on our relationship with the Lord, we will easily comprehend its value.

Jesus took extended times in separation to pray and commune with His Father. Having no home of His own, He usually went into a mountain and spent time there alone with His Father. Then He also entered into the synagogues and participated with the people in their services.

There is a powerful Old Testament Prophecy regarding the attitude we take concerning entering into God's seventh day Sabbath correctly:

Isaiah 58:13-14
13 "If you turn away your foot from the Sabbath, From doing your pleasure on My holy day, And call the Sabbath a delight, The holy day of the LORD honorable, And shall honor Him, not doing your own ways, Nor finding your own pleasure, Nor speaking your own words,
14 Then you shall delight yourself in the LORD; And I will cause you to ride on the high hills of the earth, And feed you with the heritage of Jacob your father. The mouth of the LORD has spoken."

Questions to ponder:

1. Have you come to a place of rest in your salvation?

2. How do you best describe your walk of faith, striving to rest? Or just striving?

3. Do you see the importance of "holy days"?

4. How do you respond to the "Sabbath" principles? Do you set aside any days as unto the Lord alone?

5. Do you find yourself so busy you are unable to relax and rest in God's goodness and presence?

6. If so, how will you solve the unrest this condition reveals?

Chapter 12
Light

John 8:12
Then Jesus spoke to them again, saying, "I am the light of the world. He who follows Me shall not walk in darkness, but have the light of life."

Principle

Just as the Kingdom of Darkness operates by the principle of hiding the truth, and by motivating people from behind the scenes into sin and death, the Kingdom of God operates by the principle of light, giving us the ability to see where we are going and make our own free decisions regarding the life choices we make.

The sons of God are those who walk in light and joyfully make righteous choices.

Natural light

Light is an energy source that reflects back to our eyes. Our eyes, upon receiving these light rays, are able to sort out the various colors and shapes that the light reveals. Light does not create the images. The objects themselves reflect the light rays back to our eyes. Once we see things as they really are, we are able to choose our path through them, or approach and enjoy them.

Light does not make our decisions for us. It only makes us aware of what is around us. Even so spiritual light is a spiritual awareness that helps us make better decisions than we would if we could not see spiritually.

When we walk in darkness the same things exist as before, but because of the absence of light, we cannot see them. When we cannot see things as they really are, we are likely to make poor decisions and to stumble over unseen obstacles or dangers.

Those who walk in the light are able to move through life without stumbling over what Satan would put in front of them, and at the same time become enriched by seeing and enjoying all the good things that God places in their pathway.

The Apostle Paul explained the issue by definition and principle:

Ephesians 5:13
But all things that are exposed are made manifest by the light, for whatever makes manifest is light.

The sons of God walk in light.

The concept of spiritual light reveals one of the primary ways that the Holy Spirit leads us today.

Some think that to be led of the Spirit we must be constantly hearing an inner voice of the Holy Spirit instructing us in what to do and say. But God did not create us to be empty minded robots. Instead He calls us into sonship.

Romans 8:14
For as many as are led by the Spirit of God, these are the sons of God.

There are times when God's Spirit leads through inner promptings and spiritual voices, however, most of the time He leads us through other means.

One of the primary ways He leads is through spiritual light.

Spiritual light was very important to the Psalmist. He writes:

Psalm 119:105

Your word is a lamp to my feet
And a light to my path.

Using the well known foot lamp as an illustration the Psalmist revealed a very precious truth, even for today.

Foot lamps were commonly used before the advent of flashlights. They were small oil lanterns that were held by a long cord or wire so the dim light could light the pathway. Much like the old railroad lantern, they were carried in such a way that their light would extend about six or eight feet in front and to the side.

This small circle of light would enable the bearer and those close by him to see just a couple of steps ahead of them.

The importance of this kind of light is obvious. When walking through rough terrain or near rivers, obstacles, or other dangers, the foot lamp would give light to their path, and enable them to avoid the pitfalls and dangers they would otherwise fall into or trip over.

The Psalmist declares that God's Word is like that foot lamp. It gives light to my path. It enables me to see dangers as well as the spiritual pathway to follow. With the light of the Word I can avoid evil and move ahead in safety.

Pathways

The term "path" reveals how righteousness guides us. When used as a metaphor it helps us understand the way of the Spirit. A path is a place to walk. It is a clear way through, around, and over obstacles.

In the olden times a path was also called a trail. Many people still use them. If you are a hiker you know the value of a trail. It is a way prepared for you by those who were there before, that helps you reach your destination without having to build your own way.

There are separate paths for the righteous and the sinner. It is impossible for the man who walks on the pathway of the sinner to be guided by the Spirit. It is the Spirit Himself who creates the pathway of the righteous. The man who walks on the path of righteousness is being guided by the Holy Spirit.

The man who walks in the "way" of sinners refuses the light of God. It is a way of spiritual darkness. The way of sinners is spiritual in that darkness permeates the attitude and purposes of those who walk in it.

When our eyes are evil

Jesus taught His Disciples:

Matthew 6:22-23
The lamp of the body is the eye. If therefore your eye is good, your whole body will be full of light.
23 but if your eye is bad, your whole body will be full of darkness. If therefore the light that is in you is darkness, how great is that darkness.

Not only do we need light, we need clear unobstructed sight in order to see. Just as natural sight comes through our natural eyes, spiritual sight comes through spiritual vision.

Our natural eyes have the ability to receive light rays and translate them into mental images that are recognizable to us. If our eyes are distorted, then what is seen is also distorted to us.

Jesus clearly taught us that spiritual darkness can come to us in many shades and through many distortions. We need to take heed to our ability to see clearly spiritually as well as naturally.

A prime example of this principle is given in Jesus' teaching regarding correcting offenses in other people.

Matthew 7:3-5

3 "And why do you look at the speck in your brother's eye, but do not consider the plank in your own eye?
4 "Or how can you say to your brother, `Let me remove the speck from your eye'; and look, a plank is in your own eye?
5 "Hypocrite! First remove the plank from your own eye, and then you will see clearly to remove the speck from your brother's eye."

The message is clear, our own sins and offenses cause powerful obstructions to our own spiritual vision. Before we criticize or judge another person, we must first deal with our own sight problems in order to see clearly and judge correctly.

Scripture also reveals that spiritual darkness enters our hearts and minds through incorrect motivations in our hearts. Our own selfish and sinful purposes filter the light so that our vision becomes blurred and we can't see clearly.

Spiritual attitudes are part of the make up of the spiritual walk. When we begin to move in evil motivations and attitudes we immediately lose the power of clear spiritual sight that we once had.

Some attitudes even reject the light. And other attitudes welcome it and what it reveals.

For example, a stubborn attitude will reject admonitions and clarifications regarding willfulness. Yet a teachable and humble spirit will cherish them.

Walking in the light reveals sin of every kind, including sins of spirit and attitude. It is for this reason that the Apostle John tells us that walking in the light enables us to be continually blessed with cleansing and forgiveness.

Having "good eyes" is important if we want to see what the light is revealing.

Proverbs 15:21

Folly is joy to him who is destitute of discernment,
But a man of understanding walks uprightly.

He reveals that when we walk in love, our lives are filled with light. When we walk in hatred our lives are filled with darkness.

1 John 1:5-7
5 This is the message which we have heard from Him and declare to you, that God is light and in Him is no darkness at all.
6 If we say that we have fellowship with Him, and walk in darkness, we lie and do not practice the truth.
7 But if we walk in the light as He is in the light, we have fellowship with one another, and the blood of Jesus Christ His Son cleanses us from all sin.

1 John 2:8-11
8 Again, a new commandment I write to you, which thing is true in Him and in you, because the darkness is passing away, and the true light is already shining.
9 He who says he is in the light, and hates his brother, is in darkness until now.
10 He who loves his brother abides in the light, and there is no cause for stumbling in him.
11 but he who hates his brother is in darkness and walks in darkness, and does not know where he is going, because the darkness has blinded his eyes.

Light and love

Walking in love is obeying Jesus' great commandment. This love John is speaking of is also the major character quality of the Holy Spirit. Therefore, it is impossible to walk in the Holy Spirit without involving ourselves in His basic character qualities.

This fact was so important to Paul that he revealed that even spiritual gifts, faith, and sacrifice, become useless if they are not operated in love. This issue is so important that it bears repeating, even though detailed in the previous chapter on Love.

1 Corinthians 13:1-3
1 Though I speak with the tongues of men and of angels, but have not love, I have become sounding brass or a clanging cymbal.
2 And though I have the gift of prophecy, and understand all mysteries and all knowledge, and though I have all faith, so that I could remove mountains, but have not love, I am nothing.
3 And though I bestow all my goods to feed the poor, and though I give my body to be burned, but have not love, it profits me nothing.

Therefore, we can conclude that walking in love is a necessary ingredient to our walk in the Spirit.

After we receive our initial "saving faith" the motivation behind our "living faith" must become "loving faith".

Galatians 5:6
For in Christ Jesus neither circumcision nor uncircumcision avails anything, but faith working through love.

Inner light sources

Proverbs 6:23
For the commandment is a lamp,
And the law a light;
Reproofs of instruction are the way of life.

The commandments reveal the laws and principles of God. And the process of learning and obeying them brings light into our being.

Reproofs and instruction are also ways we learn to apply those principles correctly.

Proverbs 15:32

He who disdains instruction despises his own soul,
But he who heeds rebuke gets understanding.

The light of conscience

Within the context of the various components of what can be called the "guidance system" of the Holy Spirit, "spiritual sight" and "spiritual light" are indispensable. They are both gifts of God to aid us. They are the foundation and empowerment for our godly conscience.

The conscience is a spiritual part of human makeup. It is the anchor for good character. It is our constant companion to remind us of what is good and not good.

The Greek word translated as conscience in English is "suneidesis" it means: co-perception, moral consciousness, conscience.

Webster's Dictionary defines conscience as: knowledge of ones own acts as right or wrong.

Therefore, it is the conscience that makes moral and spiritual judgments about what we do and say. It is sometimes referred to as the heart.

The Bible speaks of various conditions of human conscience.

* There is a seared conscience.

The "seared conscience" is the condition of the conscience of those who knowingly sin, and justify it to themselves until they no longer are sensitive to the message of spiritual conscience. "Searing" can also be the product of believing doctrines of demons and deceiving spirits.

A seared conscience is at times found in carnal Christians who refuse counsel, reject discipline, and walk in willful sin.

The Apostle Paul explained this as a problem of the last days:

1 Timothy 4:1-2
1 Now the Spirit expressly says that in latter times some will depart from the faith, giving heed to deceiving spirits and doctrines of demons,
2 speaking lies in hypocrisy, having their own conscience seared with a hot iron,

These are people who have knowledge of the truth, and may have even known the ways of the Lord, but through willful disobedience have seared their own conscience and end up *"giving heed to deceiving spirits and doctrines of demons."*

* There is a defiled conscience.

This is the conscience that has been polluted with defiling concepts and attitudes. It cannot operate clearly, and sees things through their own stained and many times bitter attitude.

These people are usually very critical of others.

Titus 1:15
To the pure all things are pure, but to those who are defiled and unbelieving nothing is pure; but even their mind and conscience are defiled.

* There is a cleansed conscience.

The blood of Jesus works to cleanse and purify our conscience when we are born again.

Hebrews 9:14
- how much more shall the blood of Christ, who through the eternal Spirit offered Himself without spot to God, cleanse your conscience from dead works to serve the living God?

God considers our conscience so important that He sovereignly cleanses it in order to enable us to turn from works that would lead us back toward death, so that we can serve Him acceptably.

Many believers today do not understand the value of a cleansed and clear conscience. If they did, they would do all they could to maintain it clear and undefiled, so it could remain sensitive to sin and evil.

The Apostle Paul made a clear conscience one of his primary personal pursuits.

In his defense before the Roman Governor Felix, Paul said:

Acts 24:16
- I myself always strive to have a conscience without offense toward God and men.

And in his second letter to Timothy:

2 Timothy 1:3
I thank God, whom I serve with a pure conscience,

In his second letter to the Corinthians when he sought to establish the validity of his ministry to them, he spoke again of his own conscience as the judge:

2 Corinthians 1:12
For our boasting is this: the testimony of our conscience that we conducted ourselves in the world in simplicity and godly sincerity, not with fleshly wisdom but by the grace of God, and more abundantly toward you.

When Satan is able to defile and sear our conscience, then we have no "natural" awareness of disobedience or sin. For this reason our conscience is one of his primary targets.

In order to walk in the light of the Spirit it is important to maintain our consciences pure before God. The benefit is that a Godly conscience can forget the sins of the past that have been forgiven, and at the same time shine the light on present areas of sinfulness that the Holy Spirit desires to deal with.

The Word of God is given to us to strengthen and develop a strong godly conscience. By reading and meditating often we supply strength and development of the understanding of true righteousness, which in turn establishes the foundation for a pure and godly conscience.

1 Timothy 1:5-6
5 Now the purpose of the commandment is love from a pure heart, from a good conscience, and from sincere faith,
6 from which some, having strayed, have turned aside to idle talk,

Without a good conscience our prayers are not answered.

Psalm 66:18
If I regard iniquity in my heart,
The Lord will not hear.

The answer is to respond to your conscience and bring your sin to the Lord for forgiveness and cleansing. He then will purify your conscience again.

Proverbs 28:13
He who covers his sins will not prosper,
But whoever confesses and forsakes them will have mercy.

The answer for a continual clear conscience is to actually obey the Word of God.

James 1:22-25
22 But be doers of the word, and not hearers only, deceiving yourselves.
23 For if anyone is a hearer of the word and not a doer, he is like a man observing his natural face in a mirror;

24 for he observes himself, goes away, and immediately forgets what kind of man he was.
25 But he who looks into the perfect law of liberty and continues in it, and is not a forgetful hearer but a doer of the work, this one will be blessed in what he does.

The Apostle Paul, as he talked to the Roman believers about offenses, explained that happiness comes from living with a pure conscience:

Romans 14:22
...Happy is he who does not condemn himself in what he approves.

When our conscience judges us as guilty, we need to bring the issue it reveals to Jesus for cleansing and forgiveness. As we immerse it in the Word of God and the cleansing blood of Jesus, our conscience becomes the tool of the Holy Spirit instead of the tool of the enemy by which he confuses us with either false self justification, or else outright denial of sin that exists in our lives.

Other issues

Integrity and perversity

Proverbs 11:3
3 The integrity of the upright will guide them,
But the perversity of the unfaithful will destroy them.

Righteousness and wickedness

Proverbs 11:5-6
5 The righteousness of the blameless will direct his way aright,
But the wicked will fall by his own wickedness.
6 The righteousness of the upright will deliver them,
But the unfaithful will be caught by their lust.

Proverbs 12:5
The thoughts of the righteous are right,

But the counsels of the wicked are deceitful.

(See also *Proverbs 3:1-26* and *Proverbs 4:10-27*)

Let's look at some of the attitudes and mind sets that turn us away from the light of God.

Foolishness

Proverbs 19:3
3 The foolishness of a man twists his way,
And his heart frets against the Lord.

Proverbs 14:15-16
15 The simple believes every word,
But the prudent considers well his steps.
16 A wise man fears and departs from evil,
But a fool rages and is self-confident.

Anger

Proverbs 14:17
17 A quick-tempered man acts foolishly...

Proverbs 15:18
18 A wrathful man stirs up strife...

Proverbs 14:29
29 He who is slow to wrath has great understanding,
But he who is impulsive exalts folly.

Proverbs 22:24-25
24 Make no friendship with an angry man,
And with a furious man do not go.
25 Lest you learn his way,
And set a snare for your soul.

Anger can become a way for sinful flesh to secure its own way. It justifies being violent and destructive to other people. It encourages forceful actions and releases evil in our souls.

James 1:19-20
19 So then, my beloved brethren, let every man be swift to hear, slow to speak, slow to wrath;
20 for the wrath of man does not produce the righteousness of God.

Ephesians 4:30-32
30 And do not grieve the Holy Spirit of God, by whom you were sealed for the day of redemption.
31 Let all bitterness, wrath, anger, clamor, evil speaking be put away from you, with all malice.
32 And be kind to one another, tenderhearted, forgiving one another, even as God in Christ forgave you.

Covetousness

Selfish desires can easily turn into lusts. When that happens the whole person becomes motivated by them. It is the principle by which Satan manipulates the whole world.

God's Word commands us not to covet any thing that has not been given or promised to us by God Himself. This is the true pathway of contentment.

Holy contentment is not to be confused with apathy, or laziness.

The Holy Spirit leads us to earnestly desire the things of the Spirit. We are to *"seek first the kingdom of God and his righteousness."*

By placing these things first in our hearts, the rest of what we need is added to us by God's own blessing and in His own timing. But to cultivate the desire to be wealthy is to allow ourselves to be pulled off of the pathway of the Lord.

The Apostle Paul instructed Timothy to instruct all who were desirous to be rich to consider the ramifications.

1 Timothy 6:6-10
6 Now godliness with contentment is great gain.
7 For we brought nothing into this world, and it is certain we can carry nothing out.
8 And having food and clothing, with these we shall be content.
9 But those who desire to be rich fall into temptation and a snare, and into many foolish and harmful lusts which drown men in destruction and perdition.
10 For the love of money is a root of all kinds of evil, for which some have strayed from the faith in their greediness, and pierced themselves through with many sorrows.

Covetous desires in the heart can cause us to begin again to pursue "things" rather than God, and then lead us in a pathway of error away from the pathway of the Spirit.

All these scriptural issues reveal that guidance is more than having a spiritual voice speaking to us regarding what we should and should not do. Spiritual guidance is a matter of working out the very righteousness of God through spiritual awareness and free and wise choices.

Questions to Ponder:

1. *Do you walk in God's light continually?*

2. *Are your spiritual eyes entirely good or somewhat evil?*

3. *What are the attitudes that hinder you from loving other disciples?*

4. *Do you seek first the kingdom of God, or do you seek first financial prosperity?*

5. *Is your conscience clear before God and men?*

Chapter 13
The Fear of the Lord

To fear is to believe. Knowing and fearing the Lord as a God who will judge sin in His people opens our hearts to wisdom and spiritual understanding.

Proverbs 1:7

> *7 The fear of the LORD is the beginning of knowledge,*
> *But fools despise wisdom and instruction.*

As we seek wisdom and understanding from the Lord He gives them to us. They are treasures that are not given to the apathetic.

Proverbs 2:1-5

> *1 My son, if you receive my words,*
> *And treasure my commands within you,*
> *2 So that you incline your ear to wisdom,*
> *And apply your heart to understanding;*
> *3 Yes, if you cry out for discernment,*
> *And lift up your voice for understanding,*
> *4 If you seek her as silver,*
> *And search for her as for hidden treasures;*
> *5 Then you will understand the fear of the LORD,*
> *And find the knowledge of God.*

The dictionary says that fear is *"emotion excited by threatening evil or impending pain, accompanied by a desire to avoid or escape it;"*

"Apprehension" and *"dread"* are listed as synonyms.

Another definition is *"reverence for constituted authority, especially when accompanied by obedience thereto; as, the fear of God.*

There are several words in the Hebrew language that are translated fear in your Bible. Three of them are used the most.

They are:
* *morah* - fear, dread, terror

* *yare* - affright, put in fear, to be had in reverence

* *pachad* - be startled, to fear, be afraid, stand in awe, make to shake

In the Greek language used in the New Testament, the words "*phebomai*" and "*phobos*" are used almost entirely.

Their meaning is "to be put in fear, alarm or fright; be afraid exceedingly, fear, terror."

I am sure you can recognize our modern use of the Greek word *"phobia"* that has been carried into our medical jargon. These words are used interchangeably with fearing God and other kinds of fears.

Probably the most misunderstood ingredient in the Christian walk in our day is the "Fear of God." This confusion probably exists because of the strong commands against the common fears incited by Satan.

The confusion will be healed as we understand the message of God's Grace. For, it is as we understand His Grace that we can enter into a correct fear of God.

The fear of God is one of the most important ingredients of your faith.

Those who do not walk in the fear of the Lord are constantly stumbling.

One of the natural reasons for the lack of understanding of the fear of God, comes from a lack of fear and respect for parents and elders, as well as public officials.

God established the family as the primary training ground for most of the valuable lessons of life.

Fear is an emotion excited by threatening evil or impending pain. Therefore, fear is a kind of faith, except it believes in a bad outcome.

When we sense fear we have usually accepted a message of impending danger as fairly certain.

The reason that the fear of God is such a helpful attitude is that it expresses faith and certainty about God's judgment and punishment of evildoers.

Let me use my own experience to make my point. The knowledge of sure punishment was what made me always fear my father as a young child. I had certain proofs to attach my fear to:

One was that he told me in no uncertain terms that he would make things rough for me if I was disobedient.

Two, my mother would always let me know by that fearful look in her eye that he really would do it too!

Thirdly, it seemed every time I did get into some kind of disobedience, my father would find out somehow, and things really did get pretty rough for me. So I accepted as a fact of life, that to get along in this world you needed to be obedient to the rules that were given to you.

As I grew older I began to realize that these rules were for the benefit of everyone. I realized that when we kept them, we didn't bump into each other and hurt one another.

I finally perceive these rules as guidelines for peaceful living and loving one another.

The fear of my father helped me learn that.

So it is with God our heavenly Father.

However, many Christians do not fear God. Some groups would rather use terms that are not so strong. In fact there was a tendency some years ago to replace the term in the Bible, *"the fear of God"*, for *"the reverence of God."*

I know people that are reverent but do not fear God.

Notice what the Bible says:

Psalm 33:8
Let all the earth fear the LORD;
Let all the inhabitants of the world stand in awe of Him.

Psalm 34:9
Oh, fear the LORD, you His saints!
There is no want to those who fear Him.

Verse 11-16
11 Come, you children, listen to me;
I will teach you the fear of the LORD.
12 Who is the man who desires life,
And loves many days, that he may see good?
13 Keep your tongue from evil,
And your lips from speaking deceit.
14 Depart from evil and do good;
Seek peace and pursue it.
15 The eyes of the LORD are on the righteous,
And His ears are open to their cry.
16 The face of the LORD is against those who do evil,
To cut off the remembrance of them from the earth.

Notice the components:

* The fear of the Lord is learned.

* Its fruits are to turn from evil because of the surety of God's dealings.

* The fear of God is based upon His faithfulness to punish the ungodly and to bless the godly.

Proverbs 3:7-8
7 *Do not be wise in your own eyes;*
Fear the LORD and depart from evil.
8 *It will be health to your flesh,*
And strength to your bones.

Jesus continued this Old Testament training by teaching His first disciples who they should fear:

Luke 12:4-5
4 "And I say to you, My friends, do not be afraid of those who kill the body, and after that have no more that they can do.
5 "But I will show you whom you should fear: Fear Him who, after He has killed, has power to cast into hell; yes, I say to you, fear Him!

Notice the New Testament account regarding the heart of the Church, after the persecution surrounding Stephen's death settled down, and God gave the opportunity to serve him in peace:

Acts 9:31
Then the churches throughout all Judea, Galilee, and Samaria had peace and were edified. And walking in the fear of the Lord and in the comfort of the Holy Spirit, they were multiplied.

The powerful ingredients that brought fruitfulness were: *"the fear of the Lord and the comfort of the Holy Spirit."*

The Apostle Paul taught the believers in Corinth that the promises of God were to be received by faith and not by works, yet he mentions clearly how we should receive them as far as our attitude is concerned.

2 Corinthians 7:1
Therefore, having these promises, beloved, let us cleanse ourselves from all filthiness of the flesh and spirit, perfecting holiness in the fear of God.

It is clear that those who have problems coming to a perfect or complete holiness lack the fear of the Lord.

Paul encouraged the Philippians to fear because it was God Himself who was working in them.

Philippians 2:12-13
12 Therefore, my beloved, as you have always obeyed, not as in my presence only, but now much more in my absence, work out your own salvation with fear and trembling;
13 for it is God who works in you both to will and to do for His good pleasure.

Again, it is clear that you will not work your salvation out fully if you do not fear God who is working in you.

The Apostle Peter repeats this command in his own words:

1 Peter 1:17-19
17 And if you call on the Father, who without partiality judges according to each one's work, conduct yourselves throughout the time of your stay here in fear;
18 knowing that you were not redeemed with corruptible things, like silver or gold, from your aimless conduct received by tradition from your fathers,
19 but with the precious blood of Christ, as of a lamb without blemish and without spot.

Impartation

One of the powerful aspects of God's Word is its ability to impart to us. We actually receive the Fear of God as we read the Scriptures and see the lives of those that refuse to fear Him.

It also comes through the experiences of life itself. It doesn't take many years to see the end of those that refuse counsel and neglect the ways of God.

The First Church came to some strong conclusions by reading and studying the Old Testament Scriptures. The writer of Hebrews warns those that live carelessly and take sinful advantage of God's grace to live loosely and carnally. He writes:

Hebrews 10:28-31
28 Anyone who has rejected Moses' law dies without mercy on the testimony of two or three witnesses.
29 Of how much worse punishment, do you suppose, will he be thought worthy who has trampled the Son of God underfoot, counted the blood of the covenant by which he was sanctified a common thing, and insulted the Spirit of grace?
30 For we know Him who said, "Vengeance is Mine, I will repay," says the Lord. And again, "The LORD will judge His people."
31 It is a fearful thing to fall into the hands of the living God.

Again in *Chapter 12* he says:

Hebrews 12:25-29
25 See that you do not refuse Him who speaks. For if they did not escape who refused Him who spoke on earth, much more shall we not escape if we turn away from Him who speaks from heaven,
26 whose voice then shook the earth; but now He has promised, saying, "Yet once more I shake not only the earth, but also heaven."
27 Now this, "Yet once more," indicates the removal of those things that are being shaken, as of things that are made, that the things which cannot be shaken may remain.
28 Therefore, since we are receiving a kingdom which cannot be shaken, let us have grace, by which we may serve God acceptably with reverence and godly fear.
29 For our God is a consuming fire.

Probably the greatest insight into fearing God is found in the stories of the Bible.

In them we see men and women like you and me that came in touch with a living God and were immediately changed.

Moses

We all know the story of Moses, how he stood before God amidst the shaking mountain and the smoke of His Presence. He actually heard the voice of God speak to him. His own explanation is very colorful.

Hebrews 12:21
And so terrifying was the sight that Moses said, "I am exceedingly afraid and trembling."

This helps us understand why Moses always fell on His face before the Lord when he was confronted with a situation that inferred that he was personally wrong. Just in case, he would prostrate himself before God.

Isaiah

Isaiah was man that was called to serve as a prophet of God. His life would be part of his message, as it always is.

He was given a glimpse of the Lord in His Glory.

Listen to Isaiah's own words and see if you can sense with me what the Spirit of God was imparting to him:

Isaiah 6:1-5
1 In the year that King Uzziah died, I saw the Lord sitting on a throne, high and lifted up, and the train of His robe filled the temple.
2 Above it stood seraphim; each one had six wings: with two he covered his face, with two he covered his feet, and with two he flew.
3 And one cried to another and said:

> *"Holy, holy, holy is the LORD of hosts;*
> *The whole earth is full of His glory!"*

4 And the posts of the door were shaken by the voice of him who cried out, and the house was filled with smoke.
5 So I said:

> *"Woe is me, for I am undone!*
> *Because I am a man of unclean lips,*
> *And I dwell in the midst of a people of unclean lips;*
> *For my eyes have seen the King,*
> *The LORD of hosts."*

As the terror of the Lord fell upon him, revealing that even though he was a prophet of God, his lips were still unclean. He thought he would die.

Then God responded:

Verse 6-7
6 Then one of the seraphim flew to me, having in his hand a live coal which he had taken with the tongs from the altar.
7 And he touched my mouth with it, and said:

> *"Behold, this has touched your lips;*
> *Your iniquity is taken away,*
> *And your sin purged."*

It took a coal from the heavenly altar to purge the sin that was revealed in God's presence.

It is any wonder that Isaiah could now prophecy of Jesus' birth, life and death with such accuracy?

Daniel

Daniel had many remarkable experiences with God. He had been taken captive by King Nebuchadnezar's army. He had been trained in the college of the King in Babylon. But he had never turned from following God.

The stories of his faithfulness and persecutions, like the story of being cast in the lion's den, have encouraged many to be faithful.

But notice what happened to this faithful man when God opened heaven and revealed a greater dimension of His glory than Daniel had known before:

Daniel had been fasting and was beside the river Tigris with his servants and guards.

(I take this portion from the New International Version of the Bible.)

Daniel 10:2-10
2 At that time I, Daniel, mourned for three weeks.
3 I ate no choice food; no meat or wine touched my lips; and I used no lotions at all until the three weeks were over.
4 On the twenty-fourth day of the first month, as I was standing on the bank of the great river, the Tigris,
5 I looked up and there before me was a man dressed in linen, with a belt of the finest gold round his waist.
6 His body was like chrysolite, his face like lightning, his eyes like flaming torches, his arms and legs like the gleam of burnished bronze, and his voice like the sound of a multitude.
7 I, Daniel, was the only one who saw the vision; the men with me did not see it, but such terror overwhelmed them that they fled and hid themselves.
8 So I was left alone, gazing at this great vision; I had no strength left, my face turned deathly pale and I was helpless.
9 Then I heard him speaking, and as I listened to him, I fell into a deep sleep, my face to the ground.
10 A hand touched me and set me trembling on my hands and knees.
11 He said, "Daniel, you who are highly esteemed, consider carefully the words I am about to speak to you, and stand up, for I have now been sent to you." And when he said this to me, I stood up trembling.

God continued speaking to Him regarding the future. Then:

Verses 15-19
15 While he was saying this to me, I bowed with my face towards the ground and was speechless.
16 Then one who looked like a man touched my lips, and I opened my mouth and began to speak. I said to the one standing before me, "I am overcome with anguish because of the vision, my lord, and I am helpless.
17 How can I, your servant, talk with you, my lord? My strength is gone and I can hardly breathe."
18 Again the one who looked like a man touched me and gave me strength.
19 "Do not be afraid, O man highly esteemed," he said. "Peace! Be strong now; be strong." When he spoke to me, I was strengthened and said, "Speak, my lord, since you have given me strength."

The New Testament incidents of great revelation have the same ingredients of fear and awe:

* When Jesus revealed Himself to Mary after the resurrection, she fell face down on the ground and held Him by His feet. And she had only seen Him as the gardener!

* When Jesus appeared to Saul on the road to Damascus, we find Saul (later called the Apostle Paul) laying with his face to the ground, physically blinded by the strong light he had seen.

* When John, the beloved Apostle, who leaned on Jesus' breast, the one Jesus gave charge of His mother, the one considered to be closest to Jesus of all the Apostles, now very old and banished by the government from friends and loved ones, when he saw the vision of Jesus; this John, having served Jesus faithfully, preached the Gospel fully, walked in the power of the Spirit for decades, was alone with Jesus in His Glory.

He saw Him in a vision similar to what Daniel had seen. Listen to John's own words:

Revelation 1:10-18
10 I was in the Spirit on the Lord's Day, and I heard behind me a loud voice, as of a trumpet,
11 saying, "I am the Alpha and the Omega, the First and the Last," and, "What you see, write in a book and send it to the seven churches which are in Asia: to Ephesus, to Smyrna, to Pergamos, to Thyatira, to Sardis, to Philadelphia, and to Laodicea."
12 Then I turned to see the voice that spoke with me. And having turned I saw seven golden lampstands,
13 and in the midst of the seven lampstands One like the Son of Man, clothed with a garment down to the feet and girded about the chest with a golden band.
14 His head and hair were white like wool, as white as snow, and His eyes like a flame of fire;
15 His feet were like fine brass, as if refined in a furnace, and His voice as the sound of many waters;
16 He had in His right hand seven stars, out of His mouth went a sharp two-edged sword, and His countenance was like the sun shining in its strength.
17 And when I saw Him, I fell at His feet as dead. But He laid His right hand on me, saying to me, "Do not be afraid; I am the First and the Last.

Because of these vivid descriptions of men who saw the Lord in revelation: the test of any true revelation or dream is to see if it has brought the person into the fear of the Lord or not.

The true message of God's grace brings you to love and fear God. It does not bring you into a careless lifestyle, but instead, into true holiness with righteous motivations.

Titus 2:11-14
11 For the grace of God that brings salvation has appeared to all men,
12 teaching us that, denying ungodliness and worldly lusts, we should live soberly, righteously, and godly in the present age,
13 looking for the blessed hope and glorious appearing of our great God and Savior Jesus Christ,

14 who gave Himself for us, that He might redeem us from every lawless deed and purify for Himself His own special people, zealous for good works.

Then this command is given to Titus:

Verse 15
Speak these things, exhort, and rebuke with all authority. Let no one despise you.

Questions to ponder:

1. *Do you fear the Lord?*

2. *To what degree do you fear Him?*

3. *Do you know people that do not fear God?*

4. *What is the result of not fearing God?*

Chapter 14
The Peace of God

In his Epistle to the Romans, the Apostle Paul warned the Churches about judging one another in regards to "eating and drinking". The problem he was responding to was the controversy over the Jewish commandments concerning "clean" and "unclean" foods, and that some believers were eating foods that even though they were of the correct species, before sale in the markets had been offered to idols. These were issues of strong discussion and dissension among the believers, even causing divisions among them.

In his response over this concern Paul gave us a precious and powerful understanding of the dimension of the Kingdom of God we walk in today through the Holy Spirit.

Romans 14:17
"for the kingdom of God is not eating and drinking, but righteousness and peace and joy in the Holy Spirit.

So we can clearly understand that the Kingdom of God is manifest in these three main issues.

* Righteousness

* Peace

* and Joy in the Holy Spirit

We have already discussed how "righteousness" guides our way. So let's consider how peace and joy can also help to guide us.

Remember, when we learn how to pray over things that make us anxious, we are given God's peace as a guard over our hearts and minds.

Philippians 4:6-7
6 Be anxious for nothing, but in everything by prayer and supplication, with thanksgiving, let your requests be made known to God;
7 and the peace of God, which surpasses all understanding, will guard your hearts and minds through Christ Jesus.

The word *"guard"* comes from the Greek word "phroureo", which is a military term picturing a sentry standing guard as protection against the enemy. (Spirit Filled Bible Word Wealth)

In this respect God's peace, imparted by His Spirit into our spirits, guards our hearts and minds.

Another powerful insight is given us in his Epistle to the Colossian believers regarding the process of putting off the aspects of the old nature and putting on the new. In Chapter 3 of Colossians he finalized this list of issues by commanding them to *"put on love."*

A dear friend, Greek scholar, and theologian, Dr. Bill Thweet defined the "agape" love as "the desire to seek another's highest good." This definition is powerful to remove the idea that love is first an emotional response and not a spiritual one. God's command is first spiritual and then, when firmly established as a spiritual purpose, it becomes emotional.

The command of Jesus to His disciples and to us today, is not impossible at all. It is in fact easy. It takes a decision in our minds and spirits to do everything we can for each other's highest good.

The motivation to seek each others highest good will bring us into a dimension of being "ruled" by God's peace.

Colossians 3:14-15
14 But above all these things put on love, which is the bond of perfection.
15 And let the peace of God rule in your hearts, to which also you

were called in one body; and be thankful.

The word *"rule"* speaks of being a "referee". It makes us aware by alarming us when we begin to take the wrong path or make the wrong decision.

The peace of God comes as a result of praying through anxious problems and situations. It is God's response to human need and weakness. It is a treasure!

Peace and joy move together into our lives.

This relationship of peace sets the stage for being able to "hear" the voice of God.

Being at peace enables us to hear the voice of the Lord clearly because our anxieties and fears are quieted, enabling us to recognize when He is speaking.

The first dimension of the peace of God is to reach peace with God.

Peace with God was made for us by Jesus on the cross. He literally suffered to pay all the penalty of our sins so that God could righteously be at peace with us. When we accept Jesus as our Savior through believing in Him, we spiritually move into this peaceful relationship with God.

Many new believers actually experience a great sense of peace flood into their souls as they realize that their sins are really forgiven and that their Heavenly Father is really there for them. However, there is still an even greater dimension of peace that God has in store for them that love Him.

Jesus spoke of it to His disciples at the last supper.

In John's Gospel, chapter 14 Jesus informs His disciples that He will leave them but will come to them again through the presence of the

Holy Spirit. Then He gave them the promise of a new level of peace they had not known before:

John 14:27
"Peace I leave with you, My peace I give to you; not as the world gives do I give to you. Let not your heart be troubled, neither let it be afraid."

This new level of peace would enable them to face extremely difficult circumstances without fearing or being troubled. It was Jesus' own peace given to them by impartation.

He said that His peace would not be given the way the world receives its' peace. The context reveals that His peace is to be received through the presence and power of the Holy Spirit.

He reveals that as we refuse to allow our hearts to be troubled or afraid, He will give us His peace. This helps us understand that if we allow Satan to cause us to doubt the Lord when we face difficult circumstances we will miss out on this great impartation of peace that comes from believing and drawing near to Him in times of difficulty.

Our faith and confidence give us the ability to "see" past difficult circumstance into the eternal truth of God's power and faithfulness. When we look to Him in our times of distress, Jesus gives us His own level of peace.

There is a place of peace in our storms. There is a place of peace in the midst of opposition and persecution. There is even peace available to us when we are faced with death itself. It is the gift of Jesus. It doesn't cost us anything. Yet it cost Him everything.

To His first disciples, when they were facing their greatest trial, when everything they had believed and hoped for was being destroyed and all their hopes dashed to pieces, Jesus told them that He would give them His own peace.

It is called the Peace of God. Let it rule your life.

To walk in the peace of God is to walk in the Spirit.

Questions to ponder:

1. Do you experience peace with God because of your faith in Jesus?

2. Have you ever experienced the peace of God in a time of great distress or trial?

3. Have you been able to calm your fearful and troubled heart when going through difficulties you did not understand?

4. Do you live in the peace of God, or do you experience His peace only occasionally?

5. How does a person move from fear and a troubled heart into the peace of God?

6. How does a fearful and troubled heart affect the walk in the Spirit?

Chapter 15
The voice of the Lord

The Scriptures are full of occasions when God spoke to men in super natural ways. Even today His voice speaking to His children is part of the gracious way in which He deals in human affairs.

* God spoke to Adam and Eve through His Word.

Genesis 3:8 teaches that they heard the *"sound of the Lord God walking in the garden in the cool of the day,"* This can be translated as the *"voice of the Lord in the wind of the day"*.

They were able to "hear" the voice of God.

This voice was so clear to them that they were able to converse with God.

Jesus

Jesus taught His disciples that they do hear His voice:

John 10:2-5
2 "But he who enters by the door is the shepherd of the sheep.
3 "To him the doorkeeper opens, and the sheep hear his voice; and he calls his own sheep by name and leads them out.
4 "And when he brings out his own sheep, he goes before them; and the sheep follow him, for they know his voice.
5 "Yet they will by no means follow a stranger, but will flee from him, for they do not know the voice of strangers."

Verse 14
"I am the good shepherd; and I know My sheep, and am known by My own.

Verse 16
"And other sheep I have which are not of this fold; them also I must bring, and they will hear My voice, and there will be one flock and one shepherd.

When some of the Jews did not believe Him he responded:

Verse 25-27
25 Jesus answered them, "I told you, and you do not believe. The works that I do in My Father's name, they bear witness of Me.
26 "But you do not believe, because you are not of My sheep, as I said to you.
27 "My sheep hear My voice, and I know them, and they follow Me.

According to Jesus' teaching, each true believer has the ability to "hear" His voice.

In fact He tells them this is the very reason they follow Him, because they recognize His voice above all others.

He does not say "words" but "voice". This insight reveals the personal nature of God's dealing with us.

His voice is the personal identifier that it is Him.

Knowing His voice comes from knowing Him.

OLD TESTAMENT EXAMPLES

Abraham

After Abraham had offered Isaac, and had been blessed by his sacrifice, the Lord spoke to him in renewal of the covenant of blessing.

Among the "blessings" given to him was the blessing of his seed. And the Lord told him why:

Genesis 22:18
"In your seed all the nations of the earth shall be blessed, because you have obeyed My voice."

There is no inference here that this was an audible voice. In fact the scenario has already been set by God's relationship with Adam that this was a "spiritual voice" spoken into his heart.

There is no reason to believe that God would speak differently to Abraham.

The only occasion when it is clear that He spoke to him audibly was when the Lord appeared to him in human form.

Scripture reveals that the "voice" of the Lord is consistently given into the hearts and minds of men.

Moses

In *Exodus 15* we have the story of the bitter waters of Marah.

Here we find Moses seeking the face of the Lord because of the emergency Israel was facing. In this case the Scripture teaches that Moses was "shown" a tree, and when he cast it into the bitter waters they were made sweet again by the working of God's own power.

Then God spoke to them again and said:

Exodus 15:26
"If you diligently heed the voice of the Lord your God and do what is right in His sight, give ear to His commandments and keep all His statutes, I will put none of these diseases on you which I have brought on the Egyptians. For I am the Lord who heals you."

The voice of the Lord is heard in giving *"ear to His commandments."*

In *Exodus 19-20* we find the story of how God did speak in audible sounds to the people gathered around Mount Sinai.

They had prepared themselves for three days. But when the sound of the trumpets, thunders, and then God's audible voice sounded, they became so fearful that they ran from it all. Their request to Moses was to ask him to listen to God on their behalf, and then he could talk to them and they would be able to bear it.

It was a very powerful time

Exodus 20:18-21
18 Now all the people witnessed the thunderings, the lightning flashes, the sound of the trumpet, and the mountain smoking; and when the people saw it, they trembled and stood afar off.
19 Then they said to Moses, "You speak with us, and we will hear, but let not God speak with us, lest we die."
20 And Moses said to the people, "Do not fear, for God has come to test you, and that His fear may be before you, so that you may not sin,"
21 So the people stood afar off, but Moses drew near the thick darkness where God was.

It seems that God gave a supernatural occurrence of His voice to show that we could not bear it. This explains why God chose to speak through means of prophets and others who develop their spiritual hearing. For, He continually speaks to us even today through human instrumentality as well as the written Word of Scripture.

Later in Israel's history we find God speaking to Moses in the Tabernacle, from within the Holy Place. The Scripture does not reveal whether this was audible or not. Certainly it was the voice of the Lord given in a way that Moses could identify and be certain of.

Our tradition teaches that this was an audible voice.

Numbers 7:89

Now when Moses went into the tabernacle of meeting to speak with Him, he heard the voice of One speaking to him from above the mercy seat that was on the ark of the Testimony, from between the two cherubim; thus He spoke to him.

When Aaron and Miriam withstood Moses we read God's response to them, setting the mode of God's communication with men from then on.

Numbers 12:6-8
6 *Then He said,*
"Hear now My words:
If there is a prophet among you,
I, the Lord, make Myself known to him in a vision;
I speak to him in a dream.
7 *Not so with My servant Moses;*
He is faithful in all My house.
8 *I speak with him face to face,*
Even plainly, and not in dark sayings;
And he sees the form of the Lord.
Why then were you not afraid
To speak against My servant Moses?

This revelation informs us that Moses' communion with God was very uncommon, and that God speaks to prophets through visions, dreams and dark sayings.

Joshua

Our next occasion concerning hearing God's voice was the supernatural appearance of a man believed to be Jesus Himself, appearing as the Commander of the Lord's Armies to Joshua, just before the battle for Jericho.

Joshua 5:13-15

13 And it came to pass, when Joshua was by Jericho, that he lifted his eyes and looked, and behold, a Man stood opposite him with His sword drawn in His hand. And Joshua went to Him and said to Him, "Are You for us or for our adversaries?"
14 So He said, "No, but as Commander of the army of the Lord I have now come," And Joshua fell on his face to the earth and worshiped, and said to Him, "What does my Lord say to His servant?"
16 Then the Commander of the Lord's army said to Joshua, "Take your sandal off your foot, for the place where you stand is holy." And Joshua did so.

The clear strategy given to Joshua concerning the battle of Jericho obviously came from this man. It seems that He spoke audibly just like another man would to Joshua.

This is called theologically a "pre-incarnation", meaning a pre appearing of Christ.

The Judges

In the Book of Judges we find the Lord speaking through angelic messengers. This is seen in the encounter of Gideon with the Angel of the Lord in *Judges 6:11-24.*

The Angel of the Lord is many times thought to be another appearance of Jesus.

Samuel

Then in the Book of Samuel we find God speaking to Samuel in what seemed to be an audible way.

The story, found in *1 Samuel 3:1-18* tells us how God chose to speak through the lad Samuel because of the corruption of the High Priest's family. Samuel heard God calling him and thought it was Eli the Priest. But at the third call Samuel responded directly to the Lord, *"Speak for your servant hears."*

For this reason Samuel became the Judge-Prophet of Israel.

Saul

When the Lord spoke to Saul, He spoke to him through Samuel. It is unclear whether the word for Saul came to Samuel in audible voice, or whether that was the exception.

It seems that Samuel spoke "prophetically". That is, he spoke the Word of the Lord through prophetic anointing rather than from audible words.

We can see this in the way the Lord spoke with Samuel regarding Saul's disobedience to what Samuel had commanded him in the name of the Lord.

1 Samuel 15:10-11
10 Now the word of the Lord came to Samuel, saying,
11 "I greatly regret that I have set up Saul as king...

The term *"the word of the Lord"* is used continually in Scripture to explain how God spoke to the prophets.

Peter explains this process:

2 Peter 1:20-21
20 knowing this first, that no prophecy of Scripture is of any private interpretation,
21 for prophecy never came by the will of man, but holy men of God spoke as they were moved by the Holy Spirit.

When Samuel encountered Saul after the battle with the Amalakites, he reprimanded him for disobeying this prophetic instruction:

1 Samuel 15:19 "Why then did you not obey the voice of the Lord?

Notice that Samuel called his commandment received prophetically the *"voice of the Lord"* to him.

Saul replied:

Verse 24 "I have sinned, for I have transgressed the commandment of the Lord and your words..."

From then on, except on special occasions, we find "the Word of the Lord" coming to the prophets, not as audible words, but words imparted by the Holy Spirit into the spirit of the prophets who heard them.

At the tragic end of Saul's life and kingdom we find him seeking to hear from God through Samuel who is now dead, so Saul tried to speak with Samuel through a witch.

1 Samuel 28:6
26 And when Saul inquired of the Lord, the Lord did not answer him, either by dreams or by Urim or by the prophets.

Dreams are dealt with in the next section.

Urim was an ingredient (unknown today) that was given to the High Priests' office in the time of Moses.

Tradition tells us it was carried in a pouch over the heart of the priest, upon his breastplate, and it enabled the priest to discern the will of God in a "yes or no" dimension in a matter of official enquiry.

When the priesthood lost its relationship with God the prophets seemed to take over as God's primary vehicle for communication to his people.

The Word of the Lord came to them by inner promptings that were somewhat subjective as they were tested immediately by other prophets and also a long range system of testing over "time" to determine whether or not there was a fulfillment.

This manner of testing came from God's word to Moses:

The test of fulfillment

Deuteronomy 18:21-22
21 "And if you say in your heart, 'How shall we know the word which the Lord has not spoken?'-
22 "when a prophet speaks in the name of the Lord, if the thing does not happen or come to pass, that is the thing which the Lord has not spoken; the prophet has spoken it presumptuously; you shall not be afraid of him.

If the predictions contained in the prophecy are fulfilled then the rest of the prophecy can be trusted also.

And the test of doctrinal content

Deuteronomy 13: 2-3, 5
2 "and if the sign or the wonder comes to pass, of which he spoke to you saying, 'Let us go after other gods'—which you have not known-' and let us serve them,"
3 "you shall not listen to the words of that prophet or that dreamer of dreams, for the Lord your God is testing you to know whether you love the Lord your God with all your heart and with all your soul.

5 "But that prophet or that dreamer of dreams shall be put to death because he has spoken in order to turn you away from the Lord your God,"

If the prophecy contradicts what God has already clearly said it cannot be from the Lord because He cannot lie.

Jeremiah's warning

Jeremiah revealed two other ways prophets can speak in error:

Jeremiah 23:13
I have seen folly in the prophets of Samaria:

They prophesied by Baal
And caused My people Israel to err.

In this case the prophets of Israel, headquartered at Samaria, were being moved by an evil spirit and it caused the people to live in error.

This is the same today in cults and false religions. Their messengers carry a spiritual force from evil sources, and their inspiration causes people to err.

Another level of false prophecy was that which came from the human heart and not from God's heart. It was very damaging in that it left the people thinking they were safe without seeking the Lord.

Jeremiah 23:16
Thus says the Lord of hosts;

"Do not listen to the words of the prophets who prophesy to you.
They make you worthless;
They speak a vision of their own heart,
Not from the mouth of the Lord.

Jesus

Jesus taught His Disciples regarding false prophets that were around them:

Matthew 7:15-20
15 "Beware of false prophets, who come to you in sheep's clothing, but inwardly they are ravenous wolves.
16 "You will know them by their fruits. Do men gather grapes from thornbushes or figs from thistles?
17 "Even so, every good tree bears good fruit, but a bad tree bears bad fruit.
18 "A good tree cannot bear bad fruit, nor can a bad tree bear good fruit.

19 "Every tree that does not bear good fruit is cut down and thrown into the fire.
20 "Therefore by their fruits you will know them.

Prophetic messages are to be judged by these three methods:

* Whether the message tends to lead away from holiness and serving the Lord:

* Whether predictions come to pass;

* By the fruits of the prophet himself.

"A word behind you"

Isaiah the Prophet proclaimed an unusual way in which God promised to speak to His people. This precious insight is inserted into a prophetic promise to Israel that was to come to pass when *"He will be very gracious to you..."*

We know that we are in that time of graciousness now!

Isaiah 30:21

> *Your ears shall hear a word behind you, saying,*
> *"This is the way, walk in it."*
> *Whenever you turn to the right hand*
> *Or whenever you turn to the left.*

The promise of the Lord is to give us that *"word"* that will warn us when we begin to take a wrong turn or make an error in our walk with the Lord.

He does not say that this will be an audible word. The inference is that this will be a word *"behind"* you that will speak to your own spirit, yet within our ability to hear.

Dreams

God spoke many times through dreams in Scripture.

Old Testament

Joseph

God spoke to Joseph through dreams. *(Genesis 37:5)* But Joseph's family did not know how to deal with this phenomenon. It was very difficult for them to handle. They ended up rejecting the very ministry that God had given them through Joseph in order to deliver them in the future.

Joseph was taken by his own brothers and was sold to traveling merchants who sold him to Egypt. And in the process of time, even though in prison, he developed the prophetic dimension given him and interpreted the dreams of other prisoners. (*Genesis 40:7-23)*

Then Pharaoh, the king of Egypt, dreamed regarding Egypt's future and Joseph was called in to interpret the dreams. *(Genesis 41:14-36)*

The prophetic revelation and wisdom given by Joseph was used by the Lord to promote Joseph, and use him to deliver his brothers and their families according to the dream he received as a lad, the very dream that had been rejected by his brothers.

Daniel

Daniel was given ability to interpret dreams. *(Daniel 1:17)*

Nebuchadnezzar, the King of Babylon, dreamed and Daniel revealed the dream and then interpreted it. *(Daniel 2:17-45)*

Other Prophets

Many of the prophets heard the Lord speak and saw prophetic visions through dreams.

The New Testament

The birth of Jesus

Joseph was instructed in a dream to accept Mary as his wife. *(Matthew 1:20-21)*

Peter

While in Joppa, Peter was given a dream or vision while in a trance. It was a revelation regarding God's acceptance of what the Jews considered unclean people. Through this dream the Lord opened his heart to preach to Cornelius' household even though Jewish custom forbade fellowship with gentiles. *(Acts 10:10-16)*

Paul

Paul was directed by a vision to go to Macedonia. *(Acts 16:9)*

John

The Apostle John wrote his great prophetic vision received when he was banished to the Isle of Patmos. It is called *"The Revelation"* and is part of our New Testament.

God spoke and gave instruction to men of old in this way. But it did not take the place of the more common ways of guidance. Dreams were considered only part of the way God spoke to His people.

Some dreams are not even remembered.

Job 33:14-18

14 For God may speak in one way, or in another,
Yet man does not perceive it.
15 In a dream, in a vision of the night,
When deep sleep falls upon men,
While slumbering on their beds,
16 Then He opens the ears of men,
And seals their instruction.
17 In order to turn man from his deed,
And conceal pride from man,
18 He keeps back his soul from the Pit.
And his life from perishing by the sword.

The difference in dreams to the ungodly is that they seemed to need an interpretation. However, in most of the dreams given to godly men the meaning was very clear to them. They did not need an interpreter.

Dreams, visions, and prophetic words are still given to people who walk in the Spirit. And his children know His voice and follow Him.

Questions to ponder:

1. Have you been able to distinguish the voice of the Lord from the other voices that speak to you?

2. Has the Lord spoken to you audibly?

3. Have you heard the Lord speak to you through a dream?

4. Have you experienced the occasion of a "word behind you"?

5. Have you experienced the Word of God coming alive as you read the Bible?

6. Have you experience a personal Word of God in a prophetic message given by another person?

7. How many ways has God spoken to you so that you knew His voice?

Chapter 16
Manifestations of the Spirit

The word "manifestation" comes from the Greek word "phanerosis" which is translated twice in the NKJV Bible as manifestation. It is derived from the word "phaneros" which means "evident" or "open". It describes the act of making something hidden "manifest".

The Holy Spirit, although omnipresent, is invisible to human eyes, yet He carries the power of God. Jesus said that the Spirit of God is like the wind that we cannot see unless it is discerned in its result upon physical things, like the flutter of leaves or the sound in the branches. Even so with the Spirit of God, He reveals Himself in what He does.

The Spirit becomes "manifest" to us in these following ways.

1 Corinthians 12:7-11
7 But the manifestation of the Spirit is given to each one for the profit of all:
8 for to one is given by the word of wisdom through the Spirit, to another the word of knowledge through the same Spirit,
9 to another faith by the same Spirit, to another gifts of healing by the same Spirit,
10 to another the working of miracles, to another prophecy, to another discerning of spirits, to another different kinds of tongues, to another the interpretations of tongues.
11 But one and the same Spirit works all these things, distributing to each one individually as He wills.

Seeing what the Father is doing

Jesus taught His disciples the method that He used to move by the Spirit's power in order to do things that were not normally humanly possible. It was through "seeing what the Father was doing."

We see this concept in Jesus' defense of healing on the Sabbath. The story is found in the *Gospel of John, Chapter* 5.

He was walking by the pool of Bethesda and noticed the gathering of sick and infirmed people waiting for the waters to be troubled.

Legend held that an angel occasionally came and troubled the waters, and when that occurred, the first one who was able to get into the pool would be healed.

There was a lame man lying near who had been sick for thirty eight years and could not get into the pool. Jesus saw him, and moved over to him and asked him if he wanted to be healed.

He responded that he did, but that he had no one to help him into the pool.

Jesus said to him:

John 5:8
"Rise, take up your bed and walk."

The man was instantly healed and got up and rolled up his bed and walked away.

Because this happened on the Sabbath, the people around saw the man carrying his bed and wanted to arrest him for breaking the law of the Sabbath.

He didn't know what to say, so he blamed Jesus. He said:

Verse 11
"He who made me well said to me, 'Take up your bed and walk.'"

The leaders thought that by carrying his bed on the Sabbath He was breaking the law of the Sabbath. This offended them so strongly that they paid no attention to the fact that the man had been healed after thirty eight years of illness. Incensed, they inquired who had commanded him to do this.

The man who was healed did not know who Jesus was as Jesus had withdrawn Himself from that immediate area.

Afterward Jesus found the man and said:

Verse 14
"See, you have been made well. Sin no more, lest a worse thing come upon you."

The man who was healed immediately went and told the authorities who it was that had healed him and ordered him to carry his bed on the Sabbath.

They came to arrest Jesus and plotted to kill Him because he had done a miracle on the Sabbath.

Then Jesus answered them:

Verse 17
"My Father has been working until now, and I have been working."

At this statement they became very angry, because He was calling God His Father and making Himself equal with God. (*Verse 18*)

So Jesus answered them again. And in His answer we hear the premise of how Jesus obeyed the Spirit on many occasions.

John 5:19-21
19 Then Jesus answered and said to them, "Most assuredly, I say to you the Son can do nothing of Himself, but what He sees the Father do; for what ever He does, the Son also does in like manner.
20 "For the Father loves the Son, and shows Him all things that He Himself does; and He will show Him greater works than these, that you may marvel.

21 "For as the Father raises the dead and gives life to them, even so the Son gives life to whom He will.

Verse 30
"I can of Myself do nothing. As I hear, I judge; and My judgment is righteous, because I do not seek My own will but the will of the Father who sent Me."

The practice of Jesus was to somehow *"see"* what the Father was doing, and *"hear"* what the Father was saying. Then Jesus would "do" and "say" those things.

Review

God speaks in various ways to us.

* He speaks occasionally through audible voice.

The audible voice usually came, according to the Scriptural record, in times of national emergency and to special leaders He was raising up.

* He speaks constantly through His Written Word, - causing the Holy Spirit to "quicken" the message He is bringing us through it.

* He speaks to us through "the word of the Lord".

"The word of the Lord" is the prophetic voice of the Holy Spirit that we hear from prophetic people and is confirmed in our own spirits, or we some times hear it in our own spirits from the Holy Spirit that dwells within us.

* He communicates and rules through His Peace.

The Peace of God guards our thoughts and hearts. It also gives alarm to our spiritual senses when something is amiss.

* He speaks warnings to us from outside our own spirits, "behind us", when we are making an error or taking the wrong direction.

This corrective voice of the Spirit is very comforting when we are confused in our thinking and making wrong decisions.

* He speaks through teachers and prophets.

When God speaks to us through prophetic ministry He never overrules our own personal inner witness. Instead He uses our inner witness to confirm the prophetic word that is given to us through human instrumentality.

* He speaks to us through the voice of Jesus, speaking deeply into our hearts.

This "voice of the Shepherd" that we all hear is our most valuable source of guidance. It is the ability to discern His voice at all times that will enable us to walk closest to God.

* He speaks to us through dreams and visions.

To walk in the Spirit we must walk in God's words, hearing His voice.

Questions to ponder:

1. Have you ever "seen" in the spiritual sense what the Father was about to do?

2. Has God ever spoken to you through a dream?

3. Can you remember a special time when the inner voice of the Lord confirmed to you what someone else was speaking to you about prophetically?

4. Have you experienced "the voice behind you" when you needed correction?

5. Do you recognize the voice of Jesus the Good Shepherd behind the Spirit's leadings in your life.

6. What could you do to increase your sensitivity so that you could hear His voice more often, and enjoy more assurance of the Holy Spirit?

Chapter 17
Sensing God

The development of the ability to hear and sense God's voice is one of our highest priorities. Most of what we seek from God is perceived or heard spiritually.

Let's examine the foundational truths that enable us to understand the function of hearing and seeing. Obedience to these foundational principles will renew our sensitivity to hear and perceive spiritually. And, they will also bring us to the place where God will speak to us.

Although God does not speak or reveal Himself at our whim or demand, He does come, in His own timing, to those that are in the position to hear and to perceive.

Let's examine some of these basic concepts and then seek to apply them to our lives.

The unconverted can not perceive or understand spiritual things.

Jesus explained the principle to Nicodemus:

John 3:3
Jesus answered and said to him, "Most assuredly, I say to you, unless one is born again, he cannot see the kingdom of God."

The Apostle Paul taught the same thing:

1 Corinthians 2:14
But the natural man does not receive the things of the Spirit of God, for they are foolishness to him; nor can he know them, because they are spiritually discerned.

Our sin-damaged hearts affect our ability to understand

The Bible teaches that the "mind", the "understanding", and the "heart" are affected negatively by sin.

The process of evolution (in reverse) taught by Paul in Romans includes the effect of sin on the mind and heart.

Romans 1:21-22
21 because, although they knew God, they did not glorify Him as God, nor were thankful, but became futile in their thoughts, and their foolish hearts were darkened.
22 Professing to be wise, they became fools,

Verse 24
Therefore God also gave them up to uncleanness, in the lusts of their hearts, to dishonor their bodies among themselves,

Verse 26
For this reason God gave them up to vile passions. For even their women exchanged the natural use for what is against nature.

Verse 28
And even as they did not like to retain God in their knowledge, God gave them over to a debased mind, to do those things which are not fitting;

These verses explain why men can give themselves over to sin with such abandon.

Evil works cause an evil effect on the mind.

The natural state of the mind, including the understanding, is affected very severely by sin. This "sin" includes the sin nature we inherited through Adam, and the sins of commission and omission we have all personally committed.

Key words are *"futile in their thoughts"*, *"darkened hearts"*, and *"debased minds"*.

Colossians 1:21
And you, who once were alienated and enemies in your mind by wicked works, yet now He has reconciled.

The world lives by the futile thought process.

Ephesians 4:17-19
17 This I say, therefore, and testify in the Lord, that you should no longer walk as the rest of the Gentiles walk, in the futility of their mind,
18 having their understanding darkened, being alienated from the life of God, because of the ignorance that is in them, because of the blindness of their heart;
19 who, being past feeling, have given themselves over to lewdness, to work all uncleanness with greediness.

The unconverted live in *"the futility of their mind"* and with *"their understanding darkened"*. Added to this they are *"alienated from the life of God."*

Because of this darkness, they live without sensing, or *"feeling"* God.

The loss of *"feeling"* (or *"sensitivity"* NIV) was what Jesus meant when He spoke regarding *"hearts grown dull"*. *(Matthew 13:15)*

Note again *Ephesians 4:19:*
- who, being past feeling, have given themselves over to lewdness, to work all uncleanness with greediness.

When spiritual sensitivity has been lost, only the sinful nature remains to affect our consciences and establish its' own morality.

The Biblical principle of revelation at work in those who have become Jesus' disciples, has the power to penetrate the deadness of

our souls and renew our minds.

In Matthew's Gospel we find an intimate account of Jesus, who had just finished speaking to a great multitude in parables, and then began to privately explain their meaning to the Disciples. It was then that He spoke with them about the issue of revelation.

Matthew 13:10-17
10 And the disciples came and said to Him, "Why do You speak to them in parables?"
11 He answered and said to them, "Because it has been given to you to know the mysteries of the kingdom of heaven, but to them it has not been given.
12 "For whoever has, to him more will be given, and he will have abundance; but whoever does not have, even what he has will be taken away from him.
13 "Therefore I speak to them in parables, because seeing they do not see, and hearing they do not hear, nor do they understand.
14 "And in them the prophecy of Isaiah is fulfilled, which says:

> *'Hearing you will hear and shall not understand,*
> *And seeing you will see and not perceive;*
> *15 For the hearts of this people have grown dull.*
> *Their ears are hard of hearing,*
> *And their eyes they have closed,*
> *Lest they should see with their eyes and hear with their ears,*
> *Lest they should understand with their hearts and turn,*
> *So that I should heal them.'*

16 "But blessed are your eyes for they see, and your ears for they hear;
17 "for assuredly, I say to you that many prophets and righteous men desired to see what you see, and did not see it, and to hear what you hear, and did not hear it.

Jesus clearly told his Disciples that they however did see and hear and understand.

Verse 16
"But blessed are your eyes for they see, and your ears for they hear;

The Old Testament scriptures shed light on the subject, and reveal the reason that the disciples could understand and why others could not.

THE POWER OF THE WORD OF GOD

Healing the mind through Meditation and Obedience

David taught that the Word of God received with meditation could positively affect our understanding.

Psalm 119:99-100
99 I have more understanding than all my teachers,
For Your testimonies are my meditation.
100 I understand more than the ancients,
Because I keep Your precepts.

Meditation in this context is not the religious emptying of our minds as some practice, but a filling of our thoughts with Scriptures and speaking them over to ourselves while we ponder their meaning.

Obeying them is to put them into practice in our own lives.

Decisions for righteousness

We have Scriptural examples in the lives of Daniel and the three Hebrew children that were taken captive to Babylon. The Lord supernaturally opened their minds and understandings because of their pursuit of righteousness in the choices they made.

Daniel

Daniel 1:17
As for these four young men, God gave them knowledge and skill in all

literature and wisdom; and Daniel had understanding in all visions and dreams.

Solomon

Solomon received supernatural wisdom and insight because of the right choices he made. Then later he explained to his own sons what is important to pursue in life.

The key words here are *"wisdom"* and *"understanding"*. This is important to emphasize because our present secular educational process is taken up with "knowledge", while the Holy Scriptures emphasize "wisdom". And wisdom leads to wise choices.

The benefits of a strong decision toward wisdom and understanding

Proverbs 2:1-16, 21-22
1 My son, if you receive my words,
And treasure my commands within you,
2 So that you incline your ear to wisdom,
And apply your heart to understanding;
3 Yes, if you cry out for discernment,
And lift up your voice for understanding,
4 If you seek her as silver,
And search for her as for hidden treasures;
5 Then you will understand the fear of the LORD,
And find the knowledge of God.
6 For the LORD gives wisdom;
From His mouth come knowledge and understanding;
7 He stores up sound wisdom for the upright;
He is a shield to those who walk uprightly;
8 He guards the paths of justice,
And preserves the way of His saints.
9 Then you will understand righteousness and justice,
Equity and every good path.
10 When wisdom enters your heart,
And knowledge is pleasant to your soul,

11 Discretion will preserve you;
Understanding will keep you,
12 To deliver you from the way of evil,
From the man who speaks perverse things,
13 From those who leave the paths of uprightness
To walk in the ways of darkness;
14 Who rejoice in doing evil,
And delight in the perversity of the wicked;
15 Whose ways are crooked,
And who are devious in their paths;
16 To deliver you from the immoral woman,
From the seductress who flatters with her words,

21 For the upright will dwell in the land,
And the blameless will remain in it;
22 But the wicked will be cut off from the earth,
And the unfaithful will be uprooted from it.

Proverbs 3:13-18
13 Happy is the man who finds wisdom,
And the man who gains understanding;
14 For her proceeds are better than the profits of silver,
And her gain than fine gold.
15 She is more precious than rubies,
And all the things you may desire cannot compare with her.
16 Length of days is in her right hand,
In her left hand riches and honor.
17 Her ways are ways of pleasantness,
And all her paths are peace.
18 She is a tree of life to those who take hold of her,
And happy are all who retain her.

Proverbs 4:5-9
5 Get wisdom! Get understanding!
Do not forget, nor turn away from the words of my mouth.

6 *Do not forsake her, and she will preserve you;*
Love her, and she will keep you.
7 *Wisdom is the principal thing;*
Therefore get wisdom.
And in all your getting, get understanding.
8 *Exalt her, and she will promote you;*
She will bring you honor, when you embrace her.
9 *She will place on your head an ornament of grace;*
A crown of glory she will deliver to you."

Wisdom comes from the Lord to those who pursue Him through His Word. Those like Daniel, who make decisions for righteousness and purity, open their spirits for God's Word to do even more.

Deliverance from the secular system

Wisdom is far from being a priority for our present secular educational system. Neither is understanding, or discretion, or discernment. Instead, we find ourselves among a people that is technologically advanced, yet morally bankrupt, filled with the knowledge of trivia but void of understanding.

Unfortunately most of us follow the same concept of learning we pursued in secular education as we approach the Word of God.

Even when we study, we tend to "cram" rather than "meditate".

Rather than cleansing our spirits so that we can be in an attitude to hear even what we do not want to hear, we press to know what ever we are searching for, rather than coming before Him in a disciple's spirit of submission in learning.

For this very reason a disciplined verse by verse approach to the Word of God is very valuable. Reading the Proverbs and the Psalms rewards the disciple with sharpened spiritual discernment and wisdom.

To walk in the Spirit is to walk in wisdom and understanding.

The purity principle

The best way to insure that we will be able to clearly hear the voice of God is to establish purity of heart and lifestyle.

Even though purity is not pursued primarily as a means to learn from God, it does set the stage for God to give light and revelation. This fact is seen clearly in the cases of Daniel and the three Hebrew children, and also in the Psalms of David.

The Disciples of Jesus enjoyed revelation beyond their own intellectual capacity. And it came in large part from the purity of life resulting from their complete surrender to follow Jesus.

Belonging to God is a primary key to understanding.

Jesus taught:

John 8:47
"He who is of God hears God's words; therefore you do not hear, because you are not of God."

NIV - *He who belongs to God hears what God says. The reason you do not hear is that you do not belong to God."*

In *Verses 43-44* He had just said:

NIV *43 Why is my language not clear to you? Because you are unable to hear what I say.*
44 You belong to your father, the devil, and you want to carry out your father's desire. ...

Belonging to God then is important to hearing. The degree of your surrender to Him determines the degree you belong to Him. Belonging to Him means more than just belonging once. It means to be given to Him on a continual basis.

Losing our hearing

The possibility of losing their hearing became very real to the early church. This concept is revealed in the words of Jesus given to John regarding the seven churches in Asia.

All seven churches mentioned had different problems and would enjoy different blessings at His hand. But they were all given one admonition.

Rev. 2:7, 11, 17, 29, 3:6, 13, 22
"He who has an ear, let him hear what the Spirit says to the churches."

The churches had lost the ability to hear clearly as they became strong in the flesh.

It is important to maintain our spiritual hearing so that we can be sure that we follow Him in everything we do.

Purity of heart is the answer.

Purity of heart is the result of laying down our own motives and desires, and crying out for "His Kingdom to come, and His will to be done." This must be a continual prayer and cry.

Mixture - the subtle enemy

Too often, we are a mixture of many desires. We want God, but we also have accumulated other desires and drives. Our focus moves from upon Him alone to the things He gives us. When this happens it is only one more step for it to move to other things easily. It is important to constantly seek Him above every other thing.

Purity means that there are no additives. We are simple in our focus. We have no hidden agendas with God.

Holiness is the product of purity

Hebrews 12:14
Pursue peace with all people, and holiness, without which no one will see the Lord:

Holiness affects our ability to see Him.

Purifying ourselves and cleansing our walk with Him results in Him making us usable and honorable vessels in His House.

2 Timothy 2:20-21
20 But in a great house there are not only vessels of gold and silver, but also of wood and clay, some for honor and some for dishonor.
21 Therefore if anyone cleanses himself from the latter, he will be a vessel for honor, sanctified and useful for the Master, prepared for every good work.

To walk in purity and holiness is to walk in the Spirit.

Learning from Jesus

Finally let's look at one more instruction of Jesus as to what to do for true spiritual learning. The context was Jesus explaining why He revealed things to the disciples but not to the multitude, as we studied previously.

Matthew 11:25-30
25 At that time Jesus answered and said, "I thank You, Father, Lord of heaven and earth, that You have hidden these things from the wise and prudent and have revealed them to babes.
26 "Even so, Father, for so it seemed good in Your sight.
27 "All things have been delivered to Me by My Father, and no one knows the Son except the Father. Nor does anyone know the Father except the Son, and the one to whom the Son wills to reveal Him.
28 "Come to Me, all you who labor and are heavy laden, and I will

give you rest.
29 "Take My yoke upon you and learn from Me, for I am gentle and
lowly in heart, and you will find rest for your souls.
30 "For My yoke is easy and My burden is light."

Putting on His yoke, we are able to learn directly from Him in a way that reveals His innermost character to us. This is learning that goes beyond intellect and is imparted into our hearts as well as our minds.

This is learning at its highest degree.

Walking in His yoke and learning from Him is walking in the Spirit.

Questions to ponder:

1. Are you aware of the damage sin has caused to your own ability to sense, hear, and see the issues of the Kingdom of God? Or, have you become complacent about insensitivity to God's voice?

2. Are you still trying to argue with God's Word and Spirit rather than humbly surrendering to Him in every way?

3. Are you continuing to walk sometimes in the path of the unrighteous?

4. Have you put on His yoke, or are you trying to live free from it?

5. If you have said yes to any of the above questions, what do you think will be the result of your decisions?

Chapter 18
When the Eagle refuses to fly

Psalm 139:13-16
13 For You formed my inward parts;
You covered me in my mother's womb.
14 I will praise You, for I am fearfully and wonderfully made;
Marvelous are Your works,
And that my soul knows very well.
15 My frame was not hidden from You,
When I was made in secret,
And skillfully wrought in the lowest parts of the earth.
16 Your eyes saw my substance, yet being unformed.
And in Your book they all were written,
The days fashioned for me,
When as yet there were none of them!

When David wrote this powerful psalm, he described clearly that God Himself had fashioned his body and even his inward parts. He confessed that he *was "fearfully and wonderfully made"* and that only his soul could really know that.

Like the eagle, man was created for specific purposes. The accomplishment of those purposes all hinge on man's primary calling to walk with God in constant communion and fellowship through the Spirit. When man fell out of communion with God, his true purposes were unattainable. However, when a man or woman is born of the Spirit, their opportunity to enter into the realm of spiritual communion is restored, and their opportunity to reclaim their destiny is given back to them.

The eagle is designed for flight. If he refuses to fly he becomes a misfit, for his faculties don't enable him to live like other birds and animals. Every part of his bone structure, muscles, shape, and even every feather, is designed for soaring. Even so, the person born of the Spirit is designed to walk in the Spirit. If they refuse, whether from fear and unbelief or outright rebellion, they will live unfulfilled, and face a life of carnal Christianity and being led by worldly ideals. They will look spiritually like an eagle trying to live like a common bird.

If they refuse to fly they will feast on dead things.

If they refuse to fly they will be constantly trying to be like some other bird.

If they refuse to fly they will never know the heights, or the wonderful views of God's creation. And, they will never experience soaring on the currents of the wind alone with Him.

When a Christian refuses to walk in the Spirit, he or she will never experience the joy and fulfillment that comes from living so very close to God. By refusing the walk of the Spirit they are left with only what walking in the flesh can give them.

Can they be saved? Yes, but they will suffer loss. Such great loss!

Let us refuse to remain bound by the flesh and "mount up with wings like eagles"!

Walking in the Spirit is not as difficult as our enemy tells us. Nor is living like a common bird as fulfilling as the flesh promises. There is only one true source of eternal truth. It is the voice of the same Spirit that inspired God's Holy Word. He dwells within the believer to enable, deliver, coach, nurture, and instruct.

Each step of obedience opens up another level of possibility. And each level of growth prepares us to live in greater power.

Jesus purchased the right for each of us to be full grown sons of God, and to enjoy partnering with Him in great things. Satan seeks to divert and corrupt, to kill, steal and destroy. He hates the idea that you and I would break out of our bondage. But remember, you are a child of God. And you were designed to fly. So "mount up with wings like an eagle" and walk with God in the Spirit.

Questions to ponder:

1. Do you walk consistently in the Spirit?

2. Have you learned how to "mount up"?

3. The eagle learns to mount up before it is completely developed. Are you waiting to be perfect before you try to walk in the Spirit? Or do you believe that you must walk in the Spirit so that you can become fully developed?